# A WORK OF GOD
# THROUGH CHANGED
# LIVES

MALCOLM FORD &

GILLIAN NEWHAM

# Contents

*In remembrance of Christine, the Lord's gift to me.*
*A godly wife who accompanied me on the journey for over sixty*
*years.*

*Christine Mary Ford*
*26th December 1936 - 27th June 2018*

*To the glory of God.*

# Foreword

I hope the story that you are about to read will inspire and encourage you to find faith in God or deepen your faith in God, who is vastly greater than any of us can ever imagine. This account is not about any one person in particular but is an account of what God can do through people when they surrender their lives to Him.

The prime storyteller is my father, Malcolm Ford, whose words have been brought together by our friend Gill Newham to form this book. Memories and accounts from others, who were instrumental in encouraging and challenging the vision that was given and carried out by Mum and Dad, have also been included. This vision has enabled many people to hear, see, and benefit from an abundant life-giving God. A God who became personally involved in many of the lives of those of us who were there in the beginning, and set us on journeys that prove God and find Him to be our steadfast and secure foundation. The work of Rora has gone on to bless and encourage countless people around the globe since those early years.

For me, Christine and Malcolm's eldest son, the work and vision were also about people like Jim and Molly Rowley and Joe and Beryl Maltby. They influenced and helped shape the house Church in the early days and in doing so influenced the lives of all its young people who grew up in and around Higher Whiddon farm and Rora House. These were incredibly selfless people whose focus had been that the youth should find God and find Him to be true and faithful in their lives as they had found in their own lives.

For most of my young life on the farm, and later at Rora, I was kept entertained by a horde of young people. I have numerous memories of so many people coming to stay, sometimes more than could comfortably be accommodated, that every available chair was taken. Finding a space on the floor was difficult, and on warmer evenings, hanging out of the open windows was the norm. It is fair to say that our childhood was certainly lively and unusual but filled with valuable life experiences that have served me well over the years.

When the conference ministry began in the early 1970s, we all pitched in. I can't remember if we volunteered or were coerced into it by Mum, probably the latter! But the experience of laying tables, carrying dirty food plates and cutlery from the hut to the house for washing and then taking it back to the hut was one where many memories and friendships were formed. Through the 'working together' we found something that was of lasting value, for which I am truly grateful. I know that these early experiences were not beneficial to everyone, but I found them to be life changing. I saw that life in God's world is all about what we can receive from Him and give out to others, and not just about what we can get. Giving of oneself to God and to each other in a selfless manner is at the heart of the gospel, and in the end will make a difference to those we meet on a daily basis.

I thank God for my mum and dad, for their faith and love in Him who they came to realise could, would, and should be personally involved in their lives. They gave up many things that life could offer and chose to follow the vision that God had placed in their hearts, the outcome of which is that many lives have been impacted and changed for the greater good.

As you read this account of the history and work that is Rora Christian Fellowship Trust I pray that God will impact your life and that you will be encouraged to live a life by faith and that you will be able to work out everything that God has worked in you by His death and resurrection.

*Micah 6:8 He hath shewed thee, O man, what is good; and what doth the LORD require of thee, but to do justly, and to love mercy, and to walk humbly with thy God?*

Stephen Ford

# Happy the Souls That First Believed

*Happy the souls that first believed,*
*To Jesus and each other cleaved;*
*Joined by the unction from above,*
*In mystic fellowship of love.*

*Meek, simple followers of the Lamb,*
*They lived, and spake, and thought the same!*
*Brake the commemorative bread,*
*And drank the Spirit of their Head.*

*On God they cast their every care,*
*Wrestling with God in mighty prayer*
*They claimed the grace through Jesus given,*
*By prayer they shut, and opened heaven.*

*To Jesus, they performed their vows,*
*A little church in every house;*
*They joyfully conspired to raise*
*Their ceaseless sacrifice of praise.*

*Propriety was there unknown,*
*None called what he possessed his own:*
*Where all the common blessing share*
*No selfish happiness was there.*

*With grace abundantly endued,*
*A pure, believing multitude,*
*They all were of one heart and soul,*
*And only love inspired the whole.*

*O what an age of golden days!*
*O what a choice, peculiar race!*
*Washed in the Lamb's all cleansing blood,*
*Anointed kings and priests to God!*

*Ye different sects, who all declare,*
*"Lo, here is Christ!" or, "Christ is there!"*
*Your stronger proofs divinely give,*
*And show me where the Christians live.*

*Join every soul that looks to Thee*
*In bonds of perfect charity;*
*Now, Lord, the glorious fulness give,*
*And all in all for ever live!*

Charles Wesley, London
October 20th 1779
Quoted from *Hymns of Eternal Truth* No. 68

# When an heir of salvation
# was born

"I was a farmer's son," Malcolm said, tilting his head towards the window. "I was born just eight miles up the road on a farm in Broadhempston. The farm belonged to my grandfather, but my father rented it from him. It was coming on winter, the seventh of November, when I arrived, back in 1934. Interesting, you know." Malcolm paused. "Do you remember Millie?"

We nodded. Sitting in Malcolm and Christine's lounge on that grey, April Sunday afternoon with the rain hammering against the windows, we remembered Millie; the hospitable old lady who'd fed us giant Cornish pasties when we'd first arrived at Rora back in the late 1980s.

"Well, Millie was a family friend and the local midwife, who delivered me." Malcolm stopped for a moment, perhaps remembering Millie, or perhaps remembering his farming days.

"We'd come through the war years," he continued. "I don't remember too much about it, other than they were troubled years. Tanks used to run up and down the lanes close to our farm and we could see the fires after the bombings of Plymouth in 1940 and 1941. My family worked hard during those years.

"The Ministry of Agriculture gave every farm a quota to fill and my grandfather, who'd retired early, was one of those who had to visit the farms to check that the farmers were planting, harvesting and fulfilling their given quota. Our farm was mixed: we grew some crops, and we had livestock. I can remember helping with the hand-milking. The war-agents, or inspectors as my grandfather were called, ensured that we gave our allotted amounts of milk, eggs, butter and potatoes to the Ministry of Agriculture. Of course, the Ministry paid us the going rate, but we all had a part to play in keeping the 'war-machine' fed.

"Now then, I attended the local primary school until April 1943, when at the age of eight, my parents moved me to a private Church of England prep school called Alleyn Court. For the duration of the war, the school used Bigadon House in Buckfastleigh as the army had requisitioned the school's permanent home in Westcliff-on-Sea, Essex. When the war ended in 1945, the pupils and staff all returned to Essex and I finished my preparatory education there.

"In 1948 I took the common entrance exam and passed and went on to attend King's College, Taunton. It was an Anglo-Catholic public school, but that didn't mean much to me as my family weren't really Christians. We were just the ordinary, you know, God-fearing sort of people. My mother was well involved in the local church. She was in the choir and played the organ. My grandfather, on my father's side, was a sidesman. And we'd attend the yearly Easter service and Harvest Festival. But my father didn't have much to do with the church at all.

"I left King's in the summer of 1951 when I was sixteen years old. I didn't pass any O Levels or any exams, except for my driving tests. I had a bit of a lazy brain." Malcolm laughed. "Had you read my school report, you'd probably have agreed. *Malcolm would do better if he stopped looking out of the window,* it read on more than one occasion. It was true. I never stopped looking out the window. The day I went to school was the day I wanted to leave.

"Sending me to private school stretched my parents financially. But I take my hat off to them because private education instilled disciplines and principles in me which have served as assets throughout my life.

"So, I came home to work on my father's farm, which was all I wanted to do. I was basically an ordinary farm worker, spreading dung, milking the cows and driving tractors. My father started the process of tractor-isation," said Malcolm, letting one of his many neologisms[1] roll off his tongue, "in 1941, which was earlier than most other farmers. Although I can still remember the horses. We had five big, heavy animals, who pulled the plough and planted the seed, not to mention fertilising the fields. Once my father got his first tractor, two of the tired old horses were put to rest. By the time I left school there were only a couple of horses left. I used to get up around five-thirty to feed and groom them, but that didn't last long as my father's farm was becoming increasingly mechanised.

"I still remember the steam threshing machine too; not that my father ever owned one. No! A contractor would travel around the farms in our area from mid-July to the beginning of August with his steam engine and thresher. I must admit, it was quite an event for a little lad to see the steam engine powering the thresher. I'd watch the men do the heavy work with something approaching admiration. Everyone pitched in while my mother made sure that the men were fed and watered.

"When I was eighteen I had to go and do my National Service, which meant I was gone for two years. The local tribunal advised my father that if he were to sack a man, then I could stay at home, but my father refused to do that. So, I went. And National Service benefitted me, really. As a young man under authority I learnt what it was to submit to those over me and how to follow orders. Like the disciplines that I'd learned through my schooling, understanding the role of authority in life proved an advantage after God called us to His work in 1962.

"But I'm running on ahead," Malcolm said with a wink. "Yes! I did well in National Service but came home ready to carry on working for my father. And then I met her," he said pointing to Christine who sat quietly in the armchair near the window.

For the last few years Christine's health had been deteriorating. In April 2018 she was entering the last few months of her life here on earth. Normally so chatty and full of life, Christine added few comments to our conversation.

Unlike Malcolm, Christine was not a Devonian. Born in Surrey on the twenty-sixth of December 1936 she was the eldest of three daughters born to parents who'd married later in life. Growing up in a happy home Christine initially attended a local private primary school, but later went to Latchmere Road School in

Kingston-on-Thames with her sisters Valerie and Katharine.

When Christine was eight she contracted tuberculosis. She was so ill that her father carried her everywhere. Her parents feared she would not survive the disease. Amazingly, however, she did. Which left Christine with the sense that her life had a purpose. At twelve years of age she moved to Tiffin Girls' Grammar School.

Christine's family were what people have termed, 'nominally Christian.' Her parents attended the local Anglican church and Christine went to Sunday School. At the age of fifteen she personally confirmed the baptismal promises her parents had made on her behalf when she was an infant. The local bishop was present. Laying his hands on her he prayed she might receive the Holy Spirit. Nothing appeared to change after the bishop's prayer, and Christine left feeling disappointed. In the end it was a challenging conversation she had with a friend as they walked home from their Girl Guides' meeting that made Christine realise she wasn't even a Christian. That same night she knelt beside her bed and asked Jesus to come into her life.

Leaving school after a year of A-Levels, Christine took on a series of what used to be called 'Mother's Help' jobs, followed by a short time at Norland College, before she could start nurse's training at the age of eighteen. Christine had a position at Saint Bartholomew's Hospital in Smithfield, London. While there she accompanied a friend to Capernwray Bible College in Carnforth where she heard the gospel in a fresh, new way that touched her deeply.

In 1957 Christine and three friends took a holiday in Devon.

"I'd been to the cinema in Torquay," Malcolm said with a cheeky grin. "It was late spring, May probably. Of course, it was before I was a Christian. Anyway, I was driving my car, a battered old Ford Anglia, the long way home. Few people had cars in those days as we were still coming out of the austerity of the war. Three girls were hitch-hiking on the Newton Abbot to Totnes Road. I stopped to pick them up — that was the first and the last time I ever picked up hitchhikers.

"They were staying at a place called Hope Cove, near Salcombe. Well, I'd never heard of the place. We were farmers, and in those days, farmers didn't go dashing off to such exotic places as Hope Cove. Our lives were absorbed with farming, and we were still recovering from the war years. The furthest we travelled was the fifteen miles to Torquay, which was a run of about forty minutes along quiet country lanes. Anything beyond that was like a foreign country.

"The three young ladies showed me on the map where Hope Cove was, and I delivered them safely to their destination. Christine was already at the cottage, having travelled from London by train with the luggage.

"For some reason I returned to the girls' cottage the next day, taking with me some eggs, cream, and a bottle of wine. Having delivered my gifts I promptly offered to take them out to Plymouth. It was then that romance blossomed between Christine and me. Christine will tell you it was love at first sight." Malcolm paused. "I forget the details. But we were engaged after six weeks. Is that right dear?"

Christine sat silently, shifting her feet and staring blankly into the middle distance.

Malcolm and Christine on their engagement,
1957

"It was that summer when we were dating, it must have been 1957 because we got married in '58, that we were in Paignton and there was a beach mission organised by the Brethren church. They had a big marquee where they held gospel meetings each evening. I urged Christine to go in because I knew that she was from a bit of a churchy background, although she never tried to thrust Christianity on to me.

"To this day I can't tell you what the preacher said or any of the details of that meeting. But when the preacher asked people to come forward to receive salvation, I was up, out of my chair and down the front before you could swing the barn door open. There must have been at least three or four hundred people there but I was the only one who went forward.

"Christine didn't go forward because she already had some understanding of the gospel. I, on the other hand, knew nothing. However," Malcolm raised his forefinger. "One thing was clear. I had received Jesus into my heart. If I walked out of that marquee and got knocked down by a bus, I knew that I was going to heaven.

"From then on, I started going regularly to church in Torquay, which was a bit far from us, but I'd got to know the minister at Hele Road Baptist and so that's where I went. I was still living with my parents and I used to carry my Bible under my arm when I was heading out to church. My father didn't like that, and to some degree my new faith ostracised me from the rest of the family. My father never fully accepted my position as a Christian. Mentally he wrote me out of his will, although I didn't know that until he died. He just left me his overcoat and watch," said Malcolm nodding sadly. "And he never came to know the Lord."

"Christine and I got married in March 1958 which was about ten months after we met. We married in an evangelical Anglican church in New Malden, Surrey. My parents weren't too happy about the marriage as Christine was a townie and we were a rural family. Her father was a clever man with a good job. He was the works manager for the Chrysler Dodge Lorry Division."

Malcolm and Christine on their wedding day, 8th March 1958

Malcolm and Christine on their honeymoon,
1958

After their marriage, Malcolm and Christine made their home in Devon, settling at Bow Mill Cottage, one of the cottages on Malcolm's father's farm, and Malcolm continued working for his father.

"The cottage was pretty basic," said Malcolm. "There were flagstones on the kitchen floor and a cast iron range that burned wood and coal. The kitchen sink was an old stone one, and our front door opened straight onto the farmyard. Pigs and chickens sometimes found their way through our open door. We had electricity, although initially there was no bathroom. Our toilet was in the yard, and we'd give ourselves all over-washes in front of the range. My father paid for the installation of a bathroom and inside toilet and took the cost out of my wages each week.

"My wages," said Malcolm, holding out his hand, "were twelve pounds ten shillings for an eighty-hour week.

Malcolm and Christine with their first son
Stephen, 1959

"The cottage was also small. We had just two bedrooms and the newly installed bathroom. Rats lived in the roof, probably because there was an old water mill next door where people had ground their corn back in the eighteenth and early nineteenth centuries. The mill was derelict, and the waterwheel had been pulled out, but remnants of corn kept the rats fed."

For the next three years Bow Mill Cottage was their home. The arrival of their first two children, Stephen born in 1959, and Jeremy in 1960, meant that life naturally became fuller. With a growing family and responsibilities on the farm their attendance at Hele Road Baptist in Torquay dwindled. Although Christine noted in her writings, they received regular visits of an elderly colporteur called Mr Santer.

"Small in stature, he was no more than five foot," commented Malcolm. "Mr Santer was a faithful encourager to Christine. He would arrive at the farm on his old butcher-style bicycle with a basket filled with Bibles and Christian literature. He lived in Totnes about five miles from Broadhempston, but he cycled and walked miles, visiting villages and farms. Mr Santer was a Brethren man who knew his Bible well and had heard about us from some other Christians. He usually came when I was working in the fields. He'd spend time talking and praying with Christine and she'd buy a copy of Gospel Gems from him."

Christian colporteurs were more than just pedlars taking Bibles and literature to those who couldn't easily reach a bookshop. They were, as Dwight Moody once called them, the foot-soldiers of Christian missionary work.

"My farming duties were the same as before Christine and I married," Malcolm continued. "But I began to realise that the farm could not support three men. You see, I have a brother Roger who's ten years younger than me. At that time, he was due to leave public school, and come home to the family. Naturally he would return to farming, but the farm couldn't support my father, me and my growing family, and my brother.

"So I took it upon myself to find another farm. Initially, my father accompanied me as I looked at farms that were on the market. Although he soon tired and stopped going with me. My father and I didn't really get on that well, particularly after I became a Christian. Anyway, I carried on looking until I found one for sale just outside Ashburton."

Malcolm and Christine with Stephen and
Jeremy, 1960

Malcolm and Christine with Stephen and
Jeremy, 1961

Malcolm as a baby with three older
generations

Malcolm aged 13, 1947

Christine as a baby

Christine aged 11

# 2

"Here I am, send me!"
ISAIAH 6:8

So it was that in 1961 Malcolm and Christine moved to Higher Whiddon farm and began farming independently. Located on the edge of Dartmoor, two or three miles north of Ashburton at the end of a moorland lane, the farm was a hundred and twenty acres; the same size as the farm worked by Malcolm's father.

"Although not all the ground was useful," said Malcolm. "Some of it was woodland. Farming, as an industry, was in a depressed state during the 1960s. The continued introduction of new technology, specialised fertilisers and pesticides was moving farming towards greater capacity and productivity and the factory farming that would be established in the late 1960s. Plus..." said Malcolm, holding his hand out in front of him. "I had a large mortgage on the farm that was crippling us financially and making life exceedingly difficult, and I was ill-prepared to run the business side of the farm. My father was a hardworking farmer but he had little business knowledge. He'd left school at the age of twelve due to ill-health and he struggled with writing.

My mother, as a qualified teacher, was the one with a head for business.

"In the same year as we bought the farm, we had a holiday in South Cornwall. One of the days we took the children down to the beach at Gorran Haven. The beach was deserted, except for one other couple, who didn't have their children with them. We didn't know them but the wife said to the husband, 'I believe this family are Christians.' So they came over and introduced themselves to us. We got talking, and it turned out that the husband, John, was the minister of a Baptist church in North London."

That so-called chance encounter on Gorran Haven beach was the beginning of a friendship that would impact Malcolm and Christine's lives in ways they could not imagine.

After the move to Higher Whiddon Malcolm and Christine periodically attended St Andrew's Anglican church in Ashburton, although they didn't really settle there. By the time they were expecting their third son Timothy, their church attendance had sadly lapsed. However, God had not forgotten them, and in the October of 1962, when Christine was heavily pregnant, a salesman from a local farm machinery company visited them.

"The salesman was a quiet, respectable man called George Knapman," said Malcolm drawing his breath in quickly. "He was well known to my family as he had visited my father for years, selling agricultural spares. I must have known Mr Knapman since I was about nine years old. But what I didn't know during those years was that the man was a Christian and a member of the Plymouth Brethren in Paignton. Somehow or other he'd heard that we were Christians who were struggling, and he came to encourage us to attend church again.

"The following Saturday night there came a knock at our door. We were surprised as we weren't expecting anyone. We opened the door to find an elderly couple, we'd never met, standing on the step. We duly invited them in and were introduced.

"Mr and Mrs Arthur Philp were from Honeywell farm in Ilsington, about three miles down the road. Arthur was a local preacher in the Methodist Chapel. Ilsington Methodist chapel was built on what was once a corner of one of his fields – a previous farmer having donated the land to the Methodists for the purpose of building the chapel.

"It turned out that Arthur Philp was also a friend of the salesman George Knapman who, having visited us a few days earlier, had telephoned Arthur, telling him, 'If you don't get those two back to church then they are going to be lost.' Therefore they'd come to invite us to their Sunday service the following day.

"The next morning, we made our way to the chapel in our old Mark-1 Ford Cortina Estate with the children on the back seat. The church, a simple one-storey stone structure completed in 1852, was located at the fork in a road on the south edge of the village. We parked the car and took Stephen and Jeremy in with us. It was Harvest Festival as I remember. We were warmly welcomed, and, feeling quite at home, began attending the services regularly. Little did we know that folk were praying for young people to join them.

"The chapel was popular, well-attended and quite the hub of the area. There was always a cup of tea and piece of cake available. Each Sunday a local lay preacher, who was part of a team of preachers, would visit the chapel. Even though many of them were farmers and tradesmen, (one was even a chimney sweep) these preachers all knew their Bibles well and preached down-to-earth practical sermons with a zeal and fervour that blessed us and set a hunger rising in our hearts. We'd arrive on a Sunday morning with the children in tow, settle them in the back of the car and go in, keeping an eye on them throughout the service, of course. Sunday evenings I usually went on my own, unless we could get a babysitter to watch the children, then Christine and I would go together.

"The chapel also had a choir, a young wives' group, and a thriving youth club. Mr and Mrs Philp's son Basil, along with his wife June, led the youth work. After a short time at the chapel we joined forces with Basil and June and became youth workers with the Christian Endeavour.

"Through the scriptures in Acts,[1] God began to speak to us about baptism by immersion. We had both been baptised as infants, but we sensed God was asking us to take this step as a sign of our obedience and willingness to follow Him. The Methodists didn't usually baptise adults, so we approached David Abernethy, the minister at Hele Road Baptist, who we knew well, to ask whether we could be baptised at the church by our friend John Balchin.

"David graciously agreed. Interestingly, our friends from the Methodist chapel asked us why we got baptised by immersion in a Baptist church. We weren't aware of the opportunity to be baptised by immersion amongst the Methodists. Apparently, even though John Wesley remained a Church of England minister, he had made provision for baptism by immersion amongst the Methodists."

With the birth of their fourth child Rachel in May 1964, Malcolm and Christine felt that their family was complete. They had little idea what God was going to do in their lives; all they knew was that they had a growing desire to know God more deeply.

"One winter in the early 1960s, two fresh-faced evangelists, or missioners as they used to be called, came to Devon. Both young men, Alec Passmore and David Cole, were students at Cliff College in Derbyshire, and both were full of zeal for the gospel and God's word… et cetera," said Malcolm waving his hand in front of him, to indicate that there was a lot more that could be said about these two missioners.

"I remember going out door to door one evening, delivering leaflets that advertised the forthcoming mission. It was snowing. I'd tramped through the snow to reach a bungalow about a quarter of a mile above Higher Whiddon at Hooks Cross on the edge of the tiny hamlet of Stormsdown. Knocking on the door, I handed a leaflet to a young man called Martin Williams, who I later learned remarked, 'If a man is willing to come out on a snowy night with an invite to a mission, then there must be some truth in this Christianity and we are going to attend.'

"Yes," Malcolm continued with a sigh. "Those missioners were enthusiastic and preached the gospel with a passion that touched people's lives. We would accompany them as they travelled around the Methodist chapels in Devon. One time, we took the young maid[2] who used to babysit our children to a meeting the missioners had organised in Yeoford, Mid-Devon. Pearl

Saunders was her name, and she was from my village of Broadhempston. After we moved to Higher Whiddon she'd occasionally come and stay with us. That night Pearl attended the mission in Yeoford where she got soundly saved. And our two oldest boys, Stephen and Jeremy, made their first commitment to God at the daily children's Sunshine Corner meetings. Alec and David were greatly used by God. Many a slumbering believer was reawakened to follow Christ by those missioners.

"And as for me," said Malcolm. "It was the first time I'd ever sensed the Lord speaking a specific scripture into my heart. I was sitting in the front row, on the second or third seat when the preacher read from Isaiah. *And I heard the voice of the Lord saying, "Whom shall I send, and who will go for Us?" Then I said, "Here I am! Send Me."*[3] Immediately the verse ended, my hand shot up. I didn't understand the full implications of that verse until much later, but I'd responded and asked God to send me.

"After the mission a fortnightly adult Bible Study began to meet in our farmhouse for those who wanted to study God's word. The Methodists decided to hold the study in our home as they knew we had small children and couldn't attend otherwise. We came to the study with an expectation that God was going to do new things. I guess it would have been called a desire for 'biblical holiness'. That term may sound archaic to today's younger ears and even though we didn't recognise it then either, holiness was exactly what we were longing for. We desired cleanness and the ability to live lives that were pleasing to God.

"The number of people coming to the fortnightly study grew rapidly. Pearl, who'd gone with us to the meeting in Mid Devon, was a part of the study. At the time she was working in Newton Abbot at a chemist shop called Timothy Whites. The pharmacist, who was also the manager of the shop, was a man called Jim Rowley, who according to staff gossip was a Christadelphian. Pearl had recently gone to a conference at Brunel Manor in Torquay where they had been studying the sixth chapter of the book of Ephesians. Pearl had been talking to Mr Rowley about her studies and he gave her a copy of *Sit, Walk, Stand,* a study on Ephesians by Watchman Nee. Given that Mr Rowley was a Christadelphian, Pearl was surprised at the gift of the book and a little confused. However, one of the Methodist missioners, Alec Passmore, who was in Newton Abbot visiting his mother, went into Timothy Whites. Pearl introduced him to Mr Rowley and Alec later told her that Jim was a Christian.

Jim & Molly Rowley, 1996

"Jim and his wife Molly had already left the Christadelphians and were, with another family and a few others, meeting together in the seaside village of Shaldon and seeking God. The other family they were meeting with turned out to be our near neighbours,

John Williams from Hooks Cross, who'd come along to the Cliff College mission.

"A regular speaker from the League of Prayer also came along to our fortnightly studies. Himself a farmer and Methodist man, he'd sold his farm in Cornwall and bought one in the Buckfastleigh area. During the summer he used one of his fields each year to hold a conference, which we attended. This League of Prayer man exalted us to pray for the filling of the Holy Spirit and revival in the church, and for what he termed, 'the second blessing'. We had no idea what that was. All we knew was that Jesus Christ had died for our sins and that we were going to heaven. But the idea that it was possible to receive further blessings from God merely increased our desire to know more of Him."

God was evidently nudging Malcolm and Christine forward and planting in their hearts the desire to stand before Him clean and righteous. Christine noted the unexpected arrival of a copy of *The Cross and the Switchblade* by David Wilkerson as another step towards their search to know and experience God and His power in their daily lives. The vicar who'd married Malcolm and Christine in New Malden, and led Christine's friend Mary to the Lord, must have sensed it was right to send them a copy of the book.

Malcolm had never heard of the book, let alone read it. But he had sustained an injury from a piece of farm equipment which had left him with 'housemaid's knee,' or fluid on the knee, which meant he had no choice but to sit with his leg elevated until the fluid had gone.

"It was spring as I recall," said Malcolm rubbing his knee. "I was laid up for three days. I got hold of that book and read it from cover to cover, devouring every word in it. Here was David Wilkerson, a little-known Pentecostal pastor, sensing that he should step out and follow God with the expectation that God would do miracles in people's lives, just like He had done in the Bible. Of course David Wilkerson went through many testing times before the reality of what God had spoken to Him was seen by others.

"But that book left me with questions. If David Wilkerson's experiences were real, then why weren't we seeing God do miracles like that here in Devon? If the God that David Wilkerson knew was the same God whom we profess to believe in and know, then we were missing out. We did not see people healed or delivered from evil spirits. We started seeking the Lord more fervently, crying out for Him to work in our lives, but nothing seemed to happen.

"A few months later Christine's uncle gave us a cassette tape entitled, *The Baptism of the Holy Spirit* by David Du Plessis. Like the Ephesians in Acts chapter nineteen[4], we were completely ignorant of the workings of the Holy Spirit. And we'd never heard of David Du Plessis, a South African Pentecostal minister, who we later learned was one of the key figures in what was to become known as the charismatic movement: the movement which believed that God still worked by the power of His Holy Spirit through supernatural, spiritual gifts.

"All Christine and I knew after listening to that cassette tape was that we wanted and needed God's power in our lives. At the end of his message David Du Plessis gave an invitation for those who wanted to receive the Holy Spirit to kneel and pray. Without any fuss Christine and I knelt on the cold flagstones of our kitchen floor and prayed, asking God to baptise us with His Holy Spirit.

"We waited, expecting to hear the sound of a mighty rushing wind coming through the kitchen, but nothing happened. We felt dismayed. The next night we listened to the tape again and at the invitation knelt and prayed once more. Again, nothing! We felt just the same. What should we do? We knew little of the Bible, although I did remember one verse: '*Ask, and it shall be given you; seek, and ye shall find; knock, and it shall be opened…*'[5]

"I said to Christine, 'Dear, we have asked; we have prayed and therefore we must believe that we have received by *faith*.'

"That was it. It was as simple as that. No one was with us, beside the presence of the Lord. I've since called that experience 'tears on the flagstones,' as it was there that we first truly humbled and submitted ourselves fully to the Lord. We had not known that that's what we needed to do.

"Our friendship with John and Cherry Balchin, who we'd met on the beach in Gorran Haven, continued. From afar they had nurtured us while we were at Saint Andrew's Anglican church in Ashburton, and later at Ilsington Methodist. John was the minister of Purley Baptist Church which was flourishing. The church had a great young people's work, and John and Cherry introduced us to a couple called Robin and Celia Talbot, who the church in Purley sent out as missionaries to Thailand.

"Robin and Celia were just coming to the end of their first furlough in England and preparing to return to Thailand when they came to us for a holiday. Unbeknown to us, Robin and Celia had been seeking the indwelling and empowering of the Holy Spirit, as they felt they could not return to the mission field without God's enabling power.

"Before coming to the farm, they'd attended a Full Gospel Business Men's Fellowship meeting in London where a few of the leaders had prayed for them to receive the baptism of the Holy Spirit and the gift of tongues. They weren't in our house long before they started telling us of their experiences, which was amazing because their experiences mirrored our own a few weeks earlier.

"Over our days together we prayed, and God gifted each of us with the gift of tongues. There was no pressure. No coercion. God, through His Spirit, quietly led us and began speaking to us in different ways. He spoke to me through visions which were prophetic. And Robin prophesied for the first time, telling us that God was doing a new thing, and that many people would come to us from all over the world and be blessed.

"This seemed a little difficult to believe given that we lived in a remote, isolated location on the edge of Dartmoor. We saw few people apart from our family and we hardly ever went anywhere, except to the weekly market in Newton Abbot."

# 3

# Tears upon the flagstones

'Our lives changed,' Christine wrote reflectively, after they received the baptism of the Holy Spirit. A new joy and lightness filled them. Enthusiasm and earnest commitment to God replaced the old mediocrity and discontent, and God began reshaping them.

Those around them noticed the transformation. The young people, those who were a part of the Christian Endeavour group that Malcolm and Christine led with Basil and June Philp, started asking questions. As Malcolm and Christine shared their experiences, the young people asked whether they too could receive the Holy Spirit.

"This was what we had been seeking after," said Malcolm. "Despite our ignorance, God came and filled our hearts with His Spirit which brought us fresh life. But," said Malcolm, characteristically raising a finger, "the Methodist's didn't like it.

"I remember sharing one Saturday evening at the Bible Study that met on our farm about our recent experiences. I didn't use any biblical terminology as I didn't know any then, but I shared in simplicity what God had done in our lives and the fact that He had gifted us with speaking in tongues.

"However, the gentleman who led us in our studies came to our house and advised us that if we spoke in tongues, he would leave the meeting. This was interesting, as his teaching had been a step along the way as we sought to receive more of God into our lives. The gentleman believed in the 'second blessing', which acknowledged the need for an enabling that equipped believers to live the Christian life, although, like so many, he believed that the supernatural *gifts* of the Holy Spirit ceased to be necessary after the canon of scripture was completed. But the man was respected and well-known, and word got around that we were speaking in tongues, which was an issue for many. The said gentleman removed himself from the Bible Study, and subsequently the older adults stopped attending too, which effectively closed the meeting in our home down.

"In fact the Presbyter (the leader of the local Methodist circuit in our area) phoned us up and told us we were listening to the devil who, masquerading as an angel of light, was deceiving us. This man was a businessman who lived up on Haytor and loved walking across Dartmoor. Within a week of that phone call he had died while out walking, which was sobering.

"The chapel folk were advised to have nothing to do with us. Any mention of *the baptism in the Holy Spirit,* particularly in conjunction with *speaking in tongues,* was considered heretical and divisive back then.

"What was happening to us was not happening in isolation. At a time when the denominational churches largely held the view that the Holy Spirit's role and work through supernaturally imparted gifts had ceased, some-thing new was bubbling beneath the surface. Christians across the country were talking and seeking the power of God's Spirit. Those in the Pentecostal church, which has always sought to operate in God's supernatural gift-ings, believed that the gifts of the Holy Spirit were being restored to the Christian church. Through a second work of grace after conversion, called the baptism in the Spirit, evidenced by speaking in tongues, God was equipping Christians to live as He intended them to. Mind you, I wouldn't say I believe that speaking in tongues is the primary evidence that God has filled a person with His Spirit.

"The so-called Pentecostal beliefs pressed into main-stream Protestant denominations. People were receiving the Holy Spirit, and, realising that God could and did operate in supernatural ways, they began moving in the spiritual gifts with spontaneity and diversity. Previously unknown expressions of worship entered the church alongside new forms of prayer. God was awakening His people and calling each member to be actively involved in the ministry of His church body.

"It was called the Charismatic Movement or the Charismatic Renewal, taking the Greek word, *Charismata* – grace or spiritual – gifts – to describe the various abil-ities God gave Christians through the power of His Spirit. Amongst them were words of wisdom and knowl-edge, faith and the working of miracles, prophecy, discernment, and the speaking and interpretation of tongues. It was clear God intended the spiritual gifts and modern-day miracles to be an everyday part of a believ-er's life. Some churches gladly received this new awaken-ing, while many, sadly, did not.

"We hadn't been searching for specific gifts. We'd simply asked the Lord to empower us so that we might live as He wanted us to. Considering that Christine and I were just ordinary people, we began to think that God was giving us His power because He had a purpose for our lives.

"The Christian Endeavour work was growing. Those who attended were telling their friends that something was happening. They weren't quite sure what that *something* was, but their friends came along anyway. Perhaps it was the fun we were having," said Malcolm with a smile. "The weariness of trying to keep our faith alive had gone, and we were energised. God was also starting to answer our prayers.

"The Methodists didn't appreciate our new happy-clappy singing in the services or us raising our hands in the air as we worshipped God either. It's understandable, the congregation was mainly upright elderly folk who'd been faithful members of the church all their lives. They had their traditions and local reputation to maintain.

"Not that we were always prudent. Our excessive enthusiasm was disruptive, strengthening our reputation as rebels caught up with dubious people in dubious practices. Niggling criticisms started to surface. One of the young people broke a china cup. Someone scratched the top of the piano. Meeting in the chapel on Friday evenings as we'd done before to pray, was banned.

"The church had been praying, asking the Lord to send young people and here they were. Instead of rejoicing, people complained. We couldn't understand it," said Malcolm scratching his head. "When the Lord has met you in a deeper way the complaints seem inconsequential. So I started to pray, asking God to show us what we should do. He started connecting us with others who were seeking God or encountering Him in similar ways to ourselves.

"I remember visiting Christine's cousin, Debbie Clay. Her parents, who our children referred to as Uncle Mike and Auntie Pickles, had moved from Hove to Teignmouth. They were a devout Christian family from a Brethren background. They lived plainly and weren't too popular with the rest of the family. They 'lived by faith' as it used to be termed, in other words, without a formal salary, trusting the Lord to supply all their needs. I seem to remember there was some mumblings from Christine's aunt and mother over their circumstances.

"We found Mr and Mrs Clay to be a sincere, godly couple, who yearned for a closer walk with God. There was a young man from Teignmouth Brethren assembly there when we visited. I can picture him now, leaning against the fireplace, wearing his leather jacket and looking cool. He can't have been more than eighteen. Anyway, he said to us, 'You'll be interested to hear what Mr Clay has to say.'

"Apparently, Mr Clay had come to the place in his Bible reading where the Holy Spirit was moving in power. He couldn't fully understand the meaning or implication for believers, but he did recognise that this was in some way connected with the *fresh* something that God was doing around them. As we chatted, we understood; we were a part of that *fresh* something. Although, like Mr Clay, we didn't fully grasp what it was, other than we knew it was God's Spirit.

"A few weeks later, it must have been a Saturday afternoon early in March 1967, there came a knock at our remote farmhouse door. We opened it to find the young man who'd been wearing his leather jacket at the Clay's home in Teignmouth, standing in the porch along with a group of eight or ten other young people."

Malcolm shook his head. "How they found us, I've no idea. Christine's cousin Debbie had the vaguest of instructions on how to reach us. They knew we lived down a lane on the southern edge of Dartmoor just outside Ashburton and that we worked with young people. The group before us on that Saturday afternoon were all a part of the Brethren assembly in Teignmouth. They knew that God was awakening Christians, and they wanted to be a part of that awakening. They too, were facing opposition to their deliberations in their local assembly and were out taking a walk on Dartmoor in the rain to discuss what they should do next.

"We invited the young man, Mike Coles was his name, and his friends inside. They came into our lounge and made themselves at home. One young man called Gordon lay across our settee, while a maid called Vee started playing some of the old hymns on the piano: *Turn Your Eyes upon Jesus,* and, *Just as I am,* and such like. Vee had her dog with her and he started running around all over the place. They were a bit of an unruly lot and we did find ourselves asking, whatever is going on here?

"Those young people continued coming to the farm, bringing with them a few more of their friends on each visit. Mike Coles brought his sister Val, who in turn brought her friend Faith. Pearl invited her boss, Jim Rowley and his wife Molly, who in turn invited the Williams family from Hook Cross. John and his wife didn't attend but their two children, Martin and Jennie came on occasion.

"Others heard about us and joined them: Julian Elson, who was great friends with Mike Coles, joined the group. The two of them had motorbikes which they used to strip down right on our front porch. Gordon brought Marg Pascoe who worked with him on the same farm in Chudleigh. Gordon later came to live with us and helped me on our farm. Then a young couple, Steve and Anna, came from the village of Willand in Mid-Devon on the day that they got engaged. And so, it carried on.

"We weren't doing anything, other than praying, and without the aid of mobile phones, social media and the internet," Malcolm said with a wave of his hand, "God brought people to us.

"We didn't set out to start a meeting on a Saturday night as such, it just grew organically. Some of the young people came from the Methodist chapel, although their parents weren't keen on them coming.

"Tongues were wagging. Our neighbours knew that something was going on with us and we started getting invitations from local Christians who were eager to hear our testimony. Langley and Rosemary Humphries owned a farm close to ours and invited us and several other folks over to their home one evening.

"After refreshments and a time of sharing, we settled to prayer. I, being a little naughty, opened my eyes to see a gentleman called Leslie Sutton walking around the room on his knees praying for people. It seemed strange, yet there was a genuineness in it all. Leslie was involved with the missionary organisation WEC[1] and was one of the founders of Lee Abbey, an Anglican Christian conference centre in North Devon.

"It was here that we also met a godly couple called Bob and Nora Love from Exeter. Love was their name, and love was their nature. Bob and Nora had already heard about this unconventional couple," Malcolm winked, "who were having young people in their farm-house. You can't do much that is out of the ordinary in rural Devon without others noticing and you becoming the topic of their conversation. Plus, some of the young people that Bob and Nora knew from Exeter college had made their way to our door. Returning to Exeter, they'd told Bob and Nora what was going on at Higher Whiddon.

Bob and Nora Love

"Bob and Nora came over for coffee and we started to get to know them. We met Arthur Wallis and David Lillie. Both were Plymouth Brethren men who'd become convinced of the validity of the spiritual gifts and their place in today's church. Arthur Wallis went on to become involved in what is known as the Restoration House Church Movement.

"At Bob and Nora's home in Belmont Road we met a man called Edgar Trout. He too was from the Plymouth Brethren and primarily involved in prayer ministry against satanic forces. He was a small in stature and perhaps not one you would have expected to be involved in such ministry. But he knew his God and was a giant in confidence in Him, and full of bold, strong faith. In and around the Ashburton area several witches' covens were active, and Edgar gave us counsel on how to pray for those bound by fear and demons.

"Bob and Nora also invited us to a series of meetings they were holding at Mount Pleasant, the Methodist chapel in Exeter, although it's no longer there now. Hungry to know more, we arranged for a babysitter to look after our children and headed to Exeter along with Jim and Molly and a few others. The speaker was a man called Mr North who we'd never heard of.

"The preaching was also quite different to anything we'd ever encountered. Mr North spoke with a power and authority that was unsettling. After that first evening we all thought that we wouldn't go back the next night. But deep in our beings something stirred. We used to call those depths, *the bowels of our being.* Of course, that's another archaic expression, but that's what it was. The very depths of us responding, saying yes to the Word that Mr North preached. Consequently, when the second night came around we all found ourselves back at Mount Pleasant."

Mr North, George Walter North, was a controversial figure in the '50s and early 1960s. Born in 1913 in Bethnal Green, London, he grew up with the realisation that God was calling him to be a preacher. As a young man he sought God diligently, letting the scripture be his guiding word both then, and for the rest of his life.

People called Mr North a holiness teacher, a throw-back to the teaching of the eighteenth-century Wesley brothers. He preached about the 'baptism in the Holy Spirit' as 'new birth in Christ'. Some misunderstood his teaching, thinking that he was advocating Christian perfection, whereas he simply wanted to ensure that every Christian made a genuine beginning in the Holy Spirit, encouraging each to abandon themselves to the wonders of the salvation that Christ wrought on the Cross. He preached a growing awareness of sin and repentance in each believer as they allowed God to order their lives in a way that was pleasing to Him. And in preaching the baptism of the Spirit, he highlighted the ever-increasing need for growth in conformity to the nature and ways of Christ.[2]

Mr North pastored two churches – one in Kent and a second in Bradford. He was also involved with a church in Liverpool before beginning an itinerant ministry in the late 1960s.

"I couldn't easily put into words what spoke to us from Mr North's preaching," said Malcolm patting his chest. "But as we responded, we realised that he was articulating exactly what God had done in our lives: God had given us a hunger, drawn us to Himself, cleansed us and filled us with His Spirit. By our complete surrender to Him and the power of His Spirit, we were able to obey His word and walk in His ways.

"On one occasion we arrived late to a meeting in Exeter. Mr North was already preaching and the only empty seats were, naturally, in the front row. Timidly, Christine and I made our way to the front and sat right under Mr North's nose. We were shaking in our boots a bit as he had a commanding presence when he preached. At the end he proceeded to prophesy and pray over us. I've got that prophecy[3] written down. He said that Christine and I would be a man and woman of faith.

Mr and Mrs North, 1978

"Following that series of meetings we asked Mr North to come and visit the farm. We also asked him to recommend other speakers. Arthur Wallis came, and a young man called Norman Meeten who'd been an Anglican vicar, and a delightful young carpenter called Dave Wetherley, originally from Eltham, who possessed an infectious joy that touched everyone he met. Oh, there were so many of them in those early years," Malcolm said, closing his eyes for a moment. "Men and women who'd come into this spiritual blessing and gladly came and shared God's word with us.

Norman and Jenny Meeten

"Every meeting we arranged was packed with young, and not so young people hungry to know God and receive from Him. Like sardines, they squashed into 'the posh room' as the young people called our lounge, or into our kitchen, crowded around the range. Once every chair and stool in the house was filled, the rest of the folk had to find a space on the floor. Widening our horizons, God was causing us to meet new friends who'd either received the baptism of the Holy Spirit or were eager to hear our testimonies. But lurking beneath the surface was the knowledge that the folk at Ilsington Methodist chapel were uncomfortable in our presence."

4

# Walking on the water

"We had upset the apple cart with our Methodist friends, and there was no getting the apples back onto the cart. It was clear we needed to do something," Malcolm commented with a sigh. "I guess even today that if an up-and-coming young couple, identified as potential leaders, started speaking about things outside our theological and doctrinal understanding, then perhaps we too might react as the Methodists reacted to us. But we must always be open to God and to the ways in which He chooses to work.

"It was towards the end of 1966, if my memory serves me correctly. Not only were we at variance with the people at the chapel, but we had growing challenges at the farm. We were struggling to pay the interest on our large mortgage, and farming itself was generally in a state of flux.

"I'd already been praying and asking the Lord to show us what He wanted us to do regarding our attendance at the chapel." Malcolm stopped and raised his forefinger. "You must remember that to ask such questions or to entertain thoughts of not attending the chapel was a complete misnomer. As far as we knew, there were no churches outside the main-stream denominations, and if there were, people assumed they were cults.

"One Saturday evening after the meeting at the farm, five of us gathered to pray and seek God, asking Him to guide us specifically. Christine and I were there, and three of the young people. This was something we'd never done before and we weren't sure what to expect. One of the Methodist young people, Chrissie Cornish, who was just sixteen years old at the time, prayed, 'Lord, we are going to stay here all night if needs be, until you reveal your will to us.'

"Twenty or thirty minutes later I had a vision. We five were in a boat on the water. In the far distance there was what looked like an outstretched hand. As I looked closer, I realised that it was Jesus coming towards us walking on the water. Then a soft voice spoke quietly in my ear, and I started speaking those words out loud: 'Draw up your nets, cast them on the other side of the boat. Step out of the boat and walk on the water towards Me and I will not let you sink.' We immediately knew that this was the Lord speaking to us. The table and chairs and pots and pans of our kitchen faded as the presence of the Lord consumed our hearts, minds, and souls. Deeply moved, we wanted nothing more than to obey His word. He was calling us to step out. More tears flowed on the flagstones of our kitchen as the young people, like Christine and I had done earlier, surrendered their all to God and received the baptism in the Holy Spirit.

"The prophecy continued along similar lines to what

Robin Talbot had spoken: God was going to do something new amongst us, and He would bring people to us, but we needed to lay hold of Him in faith.

"The Lord gave me further words from the scriptures: 'Do not be unequally yoked.[1] Come out from among them and be separate... and I will be a Father to you and you shall be sons and daughters to Me.[2] And, come out of her, My people, lest you take part in her sins...'[3]

"These were clear words. God was showing us that the traditional system of Ilsington Methodists, which was largely of man's making, was not and would not allow us to flourish as God intended. Although the people at the chapel loved the Lord, we knew that we were not to remain.

"God was calling us to step out. We had no idea what the consequences of such a decision would be. All we knew was that God had spoken and, whether we understood it or not, we had to obey Him. He had started working in our lives in a real and positive way by the Holy Spirit and He was asking us to walk in His way by faith. In one sense it was daunting. Shortly after we wrote a letter of resignation to the Methodists, much to the horror of those we had been in fellowship with who thought that we were deceived and had been led away from God."

By Easter 1967 Malcolm and Christine had broken links with the chapel. Christine wrote, 'It was also the first time we had a mini conference at the farm. Many friends joined us. Amongst them were the Dale and Lewis families from Leominster. All came with the same desire to know God more deeply and each one was richly blessed by Him.'

"When we left the Methodist chapel," Malcolm said, "our involvement with the Friday night Christian Endeavour group ceased, although we did advise the chapel folk that we would be hosting a separate youth club in our home on Friday evening. That youth club flourished, making us realise that we probably needed a building other than our house in which to meet.

"Out of the blue, Mike Coles gave us a call. The Red Cross in Teignmouth had an old scout type hut they wanted to sell. They were still using the building but the area it was in was due for redevelopment. Mike asked whether we were interested in buying the hut. Without a thought I said, 'Yes,' thinking it would be great for the young people — I imagined it sitting on the edge of our orchard. Gordon was living with us at the time, and Christine, Gordon, and myself arranged to go and see the hut at two o'clock the following day.

"When we saw the size of the building we thought we'd never be able to afford it. Undeterred, I asked the Red Cross representative how much they wanted? 'Well, I can't sell you the floor,' she said, 'as it's an oak dance floor.' We nodded, waiting for her to give us a figure. 'What about five pounds?' she said, 'What?' I said. 'Five pounds,' she repeated.

"Now Christine and I had no money, but it was Gordon's birthday and he had a five-pound note in his pocket which he pulled out and handed to the Red Cross lady. We couldn't take possession of the hut then but agreed to collect it when it became available.

"That was the thirteenth of November, 1967. The following day a letter arrived in the post. Accompanying the letter was a five-pound note. The writer, a lady who worked at a George Müller home in Weston-Super-

Mare, said that she wasn't sure why, but the Lord had clearly spoken to her, telling her to send us five pounds. I looked at the postmark – it read three o'clock the previous afternoon, exactly the time we were purchasing the hut.

"As we were leaving the Methodists the Lord had also given me the scripture from Hebrews chapter ten[4] concerning not neglecting meeting with other believers. Initially I wasn't quite sure how to follow this scripture. But we'd heard of a church at South Chard in Somerset and decided to go."

South Chard church had begun in 1956. It grew up in the home of a couple affectionately known as Uncle Sid and Aunty Mill who'd started a children's work in the lounge of their large home. When some of the children's parents started coming to the meeting the work quickly outgrew the lounge, and Uncle Sid converted their old coach house into a church. Originally from a Brethren background, Uncle Sid possessed a singular desire to know God. After a visiting speaker laid hands on them, he and Aunty Mill were both filled with the Holy Spirit.

From then on it was Uncle Sid's wish to see each member of the flourishing congregation fully participating in the gifts that God had given them. Such was his desire that Uncle Sid removed the pulpit from the front of the building, inviting the congregation to speak freely from the places where they sat. The Holy Spirit moved powerfully. People saw miracles of healing and they learned to trust God in their everyday lives. Uncle Sid, and those who led with him, were committed to God and His word, eager that each member of the church should grow to maturity and serve God.

"For a few months, I can't remember how many exactly, we made the journey up the A30 to Somerset to join Uncle Sid and Aunty Mill at the fellowship there. I'd get up early on a Sunday morning to milk the cows, do all the farm jobs, and then we'd get the four children into the car and head to South Chard.

"The church was extremely popular and brimming with life. I nicknamed them 'the tambourine hillbillies,' as their worship knew no bounds. One time we were singing Wesley's 'O for a Thousand Tongues.' Above the sound of our voices, I could hear this banging going on and turned to see Aunty Mill standing at the back of the church, banging the door open every time it swung shut. They used to dance too. We'd never seen anything like that before. They had a joy and enthusiasm for worshipping God that touched us.

"It was there that our Stephen, he must have been about eight at the time, was delivered from his fear of water. I remember he ran out trembling as a baptism was taking place. Uncle Sid, Christine and I prayed for him – from then on, his fear subsided.

"We used to stay for lunch; Aunty Mill's cooking was legendary. Then we'd travel home in the afternoon as I needed to milk the cows. They were a super couple, always loving, always welcoming. Our visits to the church were a real blessing. They were also God's tool to educate us in the freedom of worship and Holy Spirit-led ministry of the word. Uncle Sid came and shared at the farm once. The Lord used that couple to inspire many people to step out and start fellowships similar to South Chard.

"The church wasn't the building. This was something which we were beginning to understand. Neither was it a specific denomination, but a body of people of which Jesus was the head and God the builder. This growing revelation enabled us to see that a group of Christians meeting in a home *were* the church. This is one of the reasons I've always preferred to use the word fellowship rather than church; fellowship conveys the sense of a group of people being in fellowship with God and one another.

"In the meantime, the Friday night youth club we hosted had exploded. Each week sixty to eighty teenagers were coming to the farm. It was amazing. But it was also becoming unmanageable. Sensing that the club had served its purpose, we took the decision to bring it to an end.

"Travelling to South Chard regularly was also unsustainable. Plus, somewhere deep in my being there was a prompting. I felt a sense of responsibility towards those who had either come out of or been ostracised from their denominational churches because of their experience of the baptism in the Holy Spirit. With the finishing of the Friday night youth club, the Christians who'd been a part of that group still came over to the farm.

"And the Lord had told us not to neglect meeting together with other Christians. Did He want us to start something? A church in our house? We had no idea what this should look like, and yet God was bringing people to us. Christine and I took time to pray. I said to her, God's word says, 'Where two or three are gathered together in My name, I am there in the midst of them.'[5]

"We already had those who were coming over on a Saturday evening. We opened our home up further, for coffee and cake, or a meal and a bed. People came from everywhere. One young Yorkshire lad called Chris French, who'd moved to Okehampton to run a Christian coffee bar while he worked as a part-time builders' lad in the day, would hitchhike down on a Saturday. Another Chris, Chris Stoneman, hitchhiked from Exeter or got a lift with Julian in his beat up A50 van which had 'We live by faith,' emblazoned in gold letters down the side. One weekend Chris's older sister Shirley was sent to spy out what was going on and came to know the Lord herself.

"Pearl came each week too. She would finish her work at Timothy Whites on a Friday evening and eventually arrive with a big bag of food that Christine had asked her to bring. Often I'd pick Pearl up from the bus in the car. If I was too busy, she'd walk the mile or so from the bus stop up the lane to our house. Jim and Molly Rowley had joined us, as had the Williams family from Stormsdown, although Sunday mornings they met with Bob and Nora Love who'd started a meeting in their home at Belmont Road in Exeter.

"The young people started arriving on Friday evening after work or college, spent Saturday messing around on the farm, driving the tractors and all sorts. Then after supper we'd start praying and God would move organically, without any planning or manipulation from us. Tears fell with much repentance, and the gifts of the Spirit flowed like a waterfall, according to Chris Stoneman.

"Sunday mornings we worshipped together and broke bread in a down-to-earth manner. There was a table in the middle of the room on which the bread and wine stood. One by one each person took a portion of bread and wine, ate, drank, and prayed before returning to their seat. I guess it was a bit of an unusual way to break bread because we got known for that. Then we'd share the things that God had shown us from His word during that week or things that we were learning.

"Our four-bedroomed farmhouse was beginning to bulge at the seams as the number of people coming each weekend increased. Friday and Saturday nights our four children slept in one room while Christine and I had another bedroom. The young people came with their sleeping bags, and the girls usually slept in the other two bedrooms while the boys slept downstairs in the lounge or on the stone kitchen floor. On his first visit, Norman Meeten commented that our home reminded him of the old woman who lived in a shoe and had so many children she didn't know what to do. Young people filled every room and were literally hanging out of the windows.

"It was all very relaxed, unorthodox perhaps, and yet it had the simplicity and fragrance to it that we were beginning to recognise as the mark of the Spirit of God. By Sunday afternoon our house resumed its normal routine as the young people left to prepare for work or college the following morning.

"While we were enjoying the vibrancy of the Saturday and Sunday gatherings, watching God bring people to Himself and begin His transforming work in all our lives, the farm as a business was becoming increasingly burdensome. Our debts were escalating. We couldn't pay traders. Some came knocking on our door demanding settlements that we couldn't make. We told them that we were Christians, that we knew it was wrong to be in debt and that we would pay them as we were able. But we couldn't see a way out.

"By the beginning of 1968 we were desperate. The farm was heading towards bankruptcy. Farming had been my life; I knew nothing else. Naturally, there were two choices ahead of us: to borrow more money from the bank, or file for bankruptcy. I asked the Lord to keep me from bankruptcy, telling Him that I would trust Him."

Christine wrote that we were badly in need of wise counsel. We confided in Bob Love. One cool February day, Bob brought Mr North down to the farm. As we knelt to pray, Mr North began to speak: 'You are a good tree planted in bad ground.' So, either the ground needed purifying or we must sell up and replant ourselves in good soil. We decided to wait a week before deciding, but the following day Malcolm had a clear sense of what he had to do. He drove to the estate agent in Newton Abbot and put the farm on the market.

Whiddon Farm, 1967

# 5

# Reality sets in and the journey begins

"I knew I had to sell," said Malcolm. "I put the farmhouse, outbuildings, and something like thirty or forty acres of farmland on the market. I had it in mind to hold back the other eighty acres as an income for myself. One man came to look at the farm and said there wasn't enough land to it. We then put the farm up for public auction. But it still didn't sell, and we came away from that experience feeling somewhat embarrassed in front of the local farming community.

"But the Lord was gracious to us. We sensed that we should remain in the area and were looking at two properties, although neither were suitable. Yet, the Lord had spoken to me personally, exalting me to be a witness to my family who all lived in the area. My grandfather and father were well known. 'Kith and kin,' those were the words lodged in my heart; I was to be a testimony to my kith and kin.

"One Wednesday in March 1968, Christine and I had gone into Newton Abbot. It was market day and Christine had gone to do some shopping while I was doing some business at the bank. We'd arranged to meet outside an estate agent's office in Queen Street. One of the properties advertised in the window caught my eye – Rora House in Liverton, an attractive twenty-six roomed property, which might historically have been called a gentleman's residence. Extensively renovated in the 1920s, the house was set in six and a half acres of garden and woodland. It was on the market for eleven thousand, five hundred pounds, or seventeen thousand, five hundred pounds with some extra land from the neighbour.

"As soon as I saw it I said to Christine, who'd always been wholeheartedly with me, 'That's it, dear.' It was a much bigger property than we'd thought of buying. But that didn't deter us. We arranged to go and view it. The house was outside the village of Liverton on the edge of a small hamlet called Halford. Reached by a long, unmade road, edged by Penn Wood on one side and open fields on the other, the track gently climbed towards the house.

"As soon as I turned the car into the driveway, it was like 'Bang! It hit me: This is the place.' Christine felt just the same, and we both knew that this was the inner witness of the Holy Spirit confirming God's will to us.

Malcolm & Christine, Joe & Beryl

"We looked at the house seven times altogether. On one occasion we took some of the young people with us and prayed together, asking the Lord to guide our steps. Another time, we took a couple who were having a holiday with Bob and Nora Love in Exeter. Joe and Beryl Maltby were their names. They were living in Leicester and had met Mr North after reaching the conclusion that there must be more to Christianity than they were experiencing in their local church. Mr North had also introduced them to a church which was meeting in a grand Victorian house in the Toxteth area of Liverpool. Like us, Joe and Beryl had a small gathering in their home.

"Eventually, the estate agent pressurised us for a decision. He wanted an answer within the next twenty-four hours. Taking a step of faith we agreed to buy Rora House and shook hands to seal the agreement. With the farm unsold, how could we purchase Rora? Naturally, our decision was ludicrous. We would be moving from a struggling farm with an eight-roomed farmhouse to Rora's twenty-six. But we believed that we were following the Lord's leading, and I set sail trying to find the money.

"Rora House was owned by a lady called Mrs Angela Bigland Bradford. Mr and Mrs Bradford had lived at Rora with their family. Sadly, Mr Bradford had died three years earlier from a brain tumour and Mrs Bradford had returned to London for the sake of her four children's education.

"Even though Rora House was on the market for eleven thousand, five hundred pounds, I sensed that the Lord was encouraging me to offer a lower figure of eight thousand, five hundred. I decided to travel to London and talk to Mrs Bradford directly. On Mr North's recommendation I stayed with a couple called Pete and Joy Palmer who used to host Mr North's London meetings.

"Mrs Bradford lived near Crystal Palace. I went to her home and boldly offered her eight thousand, five hundred pounds. She laughed, saying that she couldn't take anything less than ten thousand. She told me that she had an agent managing the sale of the property, and strangely, I knew the man as he lived in the village next to Broadhempston, where I grew up.

"I returned to Devon and visited the agent, telling him about the offer I'd made to Mrs Bradford. He confirmed what Mrs Bradford had already told me: she could not sell for less than ten thousand pounds.

"I spoke to Jim and Molly Rowley, who were a part of the meeting at the farm. Together we felt that I should raise our offer to Mrs Bradford by one thousand, five hundred pounds.

"One Saturday evening Molly had a vision of us shrouded in God's light. She sensed that they should stand with us in whatever God was calling us to do. Admittedly, we didn't know what that was, but it was a confirmation to Jim and Molly that they should support us."

Malcolm waved his hand. "Before we go on, I should just mention that when I moved to Higher Whiddon I stopped using the accountant, solicitor and doctor that my family had used for years. Our family, as did many families back then, traditionally used the same professionals for all their business and medical needs. Therefore, when I came to buy Rora I didn't have a solicitor I knew to refer to.

"Instead, I picked up the Yellow Pages telephone directory and started thumbing through until I reached 'S' for solicitor. I can see it now. I let my finger run down the page as I searched for a solicitor, Mitchelmore's was the name my finger landed on, Harold Mitchelmore and Co. I'd heard of them because they were a reputable firm in Newton Abbot.

"I telephoned Mitchelmore's with the purpose of asking for a fifty percent private loan or mortgage for the purchase of Rora House. The receptionist put me through to one of Harold Mitchelmore's sons, although the son himself was quite elderly. Mr Mitchelmore was very polite and proceeded to ask me a few questions. I explained that I was selling my farm and planning to start a church.

"'What are you going to do for income,' he asked.

"I replied honestly, telling him that I didn't know, but that I wanted to buy Rora House in Liverton.

"'Oh, I know that place' he said. 'My son did his articles of clerkship, as it was formerly called, with Sir Raleigh Buller Phillpotts' law practice in London.' Sir

Phillpotts had owned Rora House before Mr and Mrs Bradford.

"Before I could ask for a loan or a mortgage Mr Mitchelmore said, 'I'll give you a fifty percent mortgage on Rora House.'

"Flabbergasted, I replaced the receiver in its cradle. The money was in place. I had twenty-six percent of the ten thousand pounds, which was not a part of the farm business, but had been set aside for the purchase of another house. A couple who were committed to the ministry that was in embryonic form at the farm, had gifted us the other twenty four percent."

Within six weeks all the finances for the purchase of Rora House were available. Mr Mitchelmore's secretary handled all the paperwork. The only time Malcolm met the solicitor was at the completion date in June 1968 when Malcolm added his signature to the papers making Rora House Malcolm and Christine's.

"Having bought Rora I thought, oh dear me, what am I going to do as I still have the farm?" Malcolm smirked. "We were young and still had so many lessons to learn. Mr North's words over us rung in our ears. 'You are a good tree planted in bad ground.' We held onto that, believing God had taken us out of the farm with its bad soil and planted us in new, good ground."

Rora House itself was basically in sound condition. Little needed to be done for the family to move in, although Malcolm did have the house rewired and the antiquated water and central heating boiler replaced. On July twenty-first, Malcolm and Christine with their four children, and the help of the young people, filled Malcolm's car, a van and two tractors and trailers with all their furniture and moved from Higher Whiddon to Rora.

"The farm was off the market. It's normal practice to sell one property before you buy another, but that hadn't happened, as provision for the purchase of Rora House was in place before the farm sold. It felt like Rora House was a completely different entity to the farm. Although I still had to maintain the farm.

"By the end of that summer, we'd cut all the corn at Higher Whiddon and the fields were lying fallow. The livestock and the farming equipment had gone. The farmhouse was clean and tidy, and the hedges trimmed. Every few days I, or sometimes Christine and I, would pop over to make sure that everything was okay. When you have a property like that, you must keep an eye on it. We knew we could leave the ground fallow through the winter but we must decide what to do by the following spring.

"That was a difficult year," said Malcolm. "I was still trying to pay the interest on the farm's mortgage. God had told us to sell the farm. We had kept a part back for ourselves. God had not told us to do that. While from a business perspective that decision may have appeared wise, after all we did have four children and a big house to look after, we were aware that we'd made a commitment to trust God to supply all our needs. In keeping a part of the land back we were not trusting him fully. We were formulating our own plan to supplement our income.

"Plus, God had told us that the farm was bad ground. If that was the case, why were we scheming to keep a part back for ourselves? In March 1969 we put the whole farm, including the land we'd held back, on the market.

"A few days later I was at Higher Whiddon when there came a knock at the door. 'You probably don't remember me, do you?' said the man standing before me. I assured him that I did. He was the one who'd come to look at the farm a year earlier but hadn't bought it. 'I see you've put the farm with all its land on the market this time,' he continued. 'I want to buy the lot for cash.'

"The sale agreed, the transaction quickly proceeded forward. By the end of April the new family had moved into Higher Whiddon and the cash from the sale paid off the mortgage on the farm and almost all our debts. We had learned a valuable lesson. When the Lord speaks, we must do exactly as He says. He was calling us to walk with Him by faith and not by sight; to live beyond human wisdom and trust Him for the provision of *all* our finances and needs."

Malcolm winked. "There's a codicil to this story. In the December of 1968 my grandfather died and left me one of his houses. I sold the house to my brother and was able to clear all the remaining debts. God had answered my prayer. I did not have to declare bankruptcy.

"We had moved to Higher Whiddon in 1961. From a farming perspective they had been hard years. We went to the farm with nothing. For those seven years, we'd scraped a living together until finally, we left with nothing. I had been a farmer. I was a farmer's son. But I realised that God had done something in me. He had taken the desire to be a farmer and to farm out of me.

He was giving us, Christine and myself, another calling, another vocation in life.

"Looking back, I see when God planted the seeds of that call in my life. He'd sent those two missioners, David Cole and Alec Passmore, from Cliff college, preaching the Word of God in the Methodist chapels in our area.

"*Whom shall I send, and who will go for Us?* One of them had read that scripture. My response, *'Here I am! Send me,'*[1] that was my commissioning. An anointing for Christine and myself for the ministry that God was beginning to lay in our lives and that would unfold at Rora."

Malcolm with Paul & Di Moss (missionaries to Hong Kong) and friends. Di's parents were Peter & Joy Pamler

# 6

# Enjoying the Lord's presence
# when tragedy struck

Stephen was nine when Malcolm and Christine moved to Rora, Jeremy eight, Timothy five, and Rachel four. After their old farmhouse, Rora was enormous and a great place to explore. But it was the grounds that drew the children the most. Neglected and long overgrown, the gardens were a child's paradise filled with slow-worms, grass snakes, crickets and all manner of butter-flies and birds who dwelt in the unkempt wilderness. Beyond the garden and through the hedge stretched Penn Wood with its trails and paths, boulders, trees, and limitless opportunities for a child's imagination to run riot.

"Our children, like all the children who've visited since, loved the space Rora gave them. Although," said Malcolm, "the grounds were a mess. The house had stood empty for three years. The neighbour used to pop through the gate that separated Rora House from Rora Farm periodically, to check that no one had broken in or stolen the lead from the roof." Malcom gave a cheeky grin. "Our neighbours got a bit of a shock when we turned up. They, Mr and Mrs McIlroy, had bought Rora Farm in 1961 with the intention of retiring to Devon for a quiet country life. Having us live next door was an adjustment. Mind you, we got on alright.

"There might not have been any lead missing from the roof, but you couldn't see the flagstones on the terrace at the front of the house for weeds, and the rockery which drops down to the first lawn was a tangled waste of plants. The lawn looked like a jungle of tall grass and the lower lawn – well! It was supposed to be a tennis court but the brambles, I have never seen the like before, they had grown out from the hedge, trailing their twisted stems through the grass like giant snakes.

"At the back of the house there was a mountain of ash, bottles, and tins. The orchard was unrecognisable and the rose garden was a rose garden in name only. Even though the old stables and coach house were barely standing, the house itself was in good condition.

"You couldn't describe Rora as grand, but in its day it would have been a comfortable holiday residence. With its bay windows and pale pink exterior it has always been attractive. When Sir Raleigh Phillpotts inherited the house in the 1920s it was just a four up, four down. He went on to renovate it to what the main house is today.

"Off the entrance hall is the lounge with its beautiful oak floor. That oak came from the Powderham Castle Estate fifteen or so miles up the road. Sir Raleigh's grandfather was the forester on the castle estate. When Sir Raleigh was young, his grandfather gifted him with the cut and seasoned oak, telling his grandson to use it in the house he would buy later in life, and that's what he done," said Malcolm, slipping into Devonian grammar.

"Sir Raleigh's employees would come down for weekends. Opening the dividing doors to enlarge the lounge, they'd party and dance into the small hours. Beyond the so-called smaller lounge was a summer breakfast area. In truth, this was an icy wind-trap of a place which we quickly enclosed. At the back of the house was the kitchen with its oil-fired Aga range. Off the kitchen was the breakfast room which led to the scullery.

"Upstairs were four large bedrooms, complete with adjacent dressing rooms and cloakrooms. There were two bathrooms which in the 1920s' world would have been luxurious. Across the top of the house ran the attic rooms which housed the servants."

Before moving to Rora Malcolm and Christine had invited Pearl Saunders to live with them at the farm. God had already spoken to Pearl at one Sunday evening meeting, calling her to become a missionary, to which she responded by applying to the WEC Missionary Training College in Glasgow. Following her acceptance, Pearl was preparing to give in her notice at Timothy Whites in Newton Abbot and move to Scotland the following January when Malcolm and Christine's request came. The move to Higher Whiddon, and subsequently Rora, felt like a natural next step to Pearl.

"After we moved to Rora, Christine quite simply told Pearl to get a bucket and start cleaning. The two of them cleaned the whole house from top to bottom, washing walls, windows, every scrap of paintwork, and all the floors.

"Apart from Pearl and the children we were on our

own. We got to work, just doing the next job, which was largely tidying the place up and working in the grounds. As you know, during that first year, we were also still carrying the burden of the farm which was unsold. Yet underlying it all was a sense of peace, which I can hardly explain.

"Young people came as they had done at the farm, arriving on a Friday evening and leaving on Sunday afternoon. Most of them stayed in the attic rooms. Mike Coles and his great friend Julian Elson were amongst them. The two of them used to stay up late into the night having deep, meaningful conversations.

"We gathered as we had before with simplicity, singing songs and sharing scriptures. Mr North tended to come once a month, and Norman Meeten on occasion too. Jim and Molly in their own quiet, dignified way were faithfully supportive.

"Numbers were increasing. Soon there were over thirty young people coming each weekend. We met in the lounge, opening the partition doors as needed so we could fit more people in. At those times our hearts were filled with a fervour to love God with every fibre of our being. Acts chapter one, the second part of verse eight, was a scripture that was frequently on our lips, *"You will be witnesses to Me in Jerusalem and in all Judea and Samaria, and to the end of the earth."* God would cause us to be witnesses in the place we were and to the end of the earth. That was an astonishing thought.

"The presence of the Lord amongst us was almost tangible. He was opening people's eyes to the living power of the supernatural seed He'd placed in our lives, and that seed was steadily transforming our lives and minds. We simply wanted to walk with Him *each day*, listening to Him and following His word. The passion we experienced in our worship together spilled over into practical tasks. People would ask what they could do. We'd place a shovel or a hoe in their hands and point them to the garden. No one said, 'I want to do this, or I want to do that.' People were happy to get on with the job at hand and saw the chopping down of brambles and the pulling of weeds as much a part of their worship to God as the singing of a Wesley hymn.

"Even though we had bare boards in most rooms and little crockery in the kitchen, we opened the house to visitors. We felt hospitality was to be one of the cornerstones of the house. People would come for a cup of tea and a biscuit or they'd arrive at a mealtime which put pressure on Christine, but she always found a way to make a meal stretch for a few more hungry stomachs. Others came from further afield for a holiday. While some, propelled by curiosity, would come to a halt at the bottom of the lane, wondering what sort of strangeness they'd find at the top. But word travelled fast: *'Malcolm and Christine Ford have a home on the edge of Dartmoor that is open for holidays.'* Not that *we* were the attraction. No! It was the awakening. What God was working in our lives and the lives of those who met with us was a part of something that was happening across the country. God was awakening believers and non-believers to the realities of the Christian gospel.

"*That* awakening drew people together, and it drew people to Rora. They came and stayed as they felt led by the Lord. Perhaps for a few days off, perhaps for longer. Some came to help tidy up. Dave Wetherley from Eltham spent three months dividing up some of the larger upstairs rooms so that we had more bedrooms to accommodate the growing number of guests. People came when we had visiting speakers like Mr North or Norman Meeten. We didn't advertise. We didn't even need to say anything, because those who visited spoke of the encouragements God had given them at Rora, which in turn brought more visitors.

"Christine and I vowed not to charge people to stay at Rora. God had asked us to trust Him to supply all our financial needs, and that's what we were doing, especially as we watched the men who stood before us: Mr North, Norman Meeten, and Dave Wetherley. Seeing them follow God, proving His faithfulness in every aspect of their lives was inspiring. They had given everything to God, and still they sought to continually surrender to Him.

Malcolm and Christine

"They knew the reality of God in their hearts. Of course, we all need money to live, I am not denying that, and we cannot walk in a way that God has not called us to. But being willing to say, 'Lord, I will trust You to supply what we need when we need it,' takes a step of faith that causes us to walk a road whereby we must draw closer to God.

"When I was a young Christian who hardly knew God, Mr North gave me some sound advice: 'Read your Bible, boy,' he said. And I've read my Bible. I've let God's word enter my life and dwell in my heart. I've listened to renowned preachers and allowed the Holy Spirit living in me to teach me truth and bring God's transforming power into my heart and mind. Although I didn't recognise it then, these were tenets God was starting to set in the lives of both Christine and I as we settled at Rora.

"ON THE TENTH of December 1968 tragedy hit us. Two policemen arrived at Rora. Julian, who was still staying with us in one of the attic rooms, had been on his way to a meeting at the home of a family from the Teignmouth Gospel Hall, when a car driven by two naval men clipped the back wheel of his motorbike as he was turning right. Thrown into the air, Julian landed on the car's bonnet and died instantly. Stunned, we couldn't believe it. Julian was just twenty years old.

"He was engaged to Vee, who'd visited the farm that first Saturday afternoon with the young people. She was in Teignmouth, attending the same meeting that Julian had been going to. I rang to say that I was going over, but the police arrived before I got there. Naturally, Vee was devastated and returned to Rora with us where Christine sought to comfort her.

"Julian's funeral was held at the local Anglican church in Kingsteignton where his family lived. We stood in that cold building, our knees almost buckling beneath us. We were young, starting afresh, and unprepared for such devastation. It was hard to believe that Julian, with his dry wit that left him curled up on a chair with laughter, was gone. Mike Coles described him as one who was born with half a smile on his face.

"A few weeks later we had a thanksgiving service for Julian in the lounge at Rora. Arthur Wallis spoke to a packed room. Vee was our pianist. One of the hymns someone chose Vee couldn't play, so a young man who'd been a friend of Julian's came forward. He played with a gusto that set our hearts on fire. We sang at the tops of voices which must have nearly raised the roof. George Santer was the name of that young man. He was from Totnes, and his father was the colporteur who had visited Christine when we were at Bow Mill Farm."

# 7

# Happy the souls that first believed

## CHARLES WESLEY

"After the farm sold in March 1969 it felt like God had given us a clean slate. We were able to focus completely on Him and Rora. Pearl had left us in the January to go to Bible College in Glasgow, so it was just Christine, myself, and the children in the house. Although many of the young people continued staying at the weekends.

"We were a motley crew of young Christians, inexperienced in God and ministry, yet part of something that God had initiated. A group of young people from Newton Abbot Grammar School's Christian Union who had come to the Lord found us out and joined the fellowship. Together we shared a growing love for His word, and an appreciation of His holiness which led us to humbly approach Him in repentance with an on-going desire for righteousness.

"Whether in worship, fellowship, prayer, or the practical aspects of life, we encountered the indwelling of the Spirit in one another which made us audacious in prayer and faith.

"As we grew, a verse of scripture became impressed

on my heart: 'Where there is no vision, the people perish.'[1] Our meetings were fluid, perhaps even a little disorganised. I was aware that we needed a measure of orderliness. We needed to know who we were and where we were going. In no way did we want to curtail God's movements or the spontaneity that encouraged each member to contribute. But we did need to articulate our spiritual foundations and define our biblical understanding of the church meeting in a *house*, to ensure that we met in a manner that was honouring to God.

"I had been reading Watchman Nee's book, *The Normal Christian Church Life*. Parts of his chapter on 'The Basis of Union and Division' really got me thinking, and I prayerfully began mulling over the scriptures Nee cited as relevant foundational elements of the church.

"I began looking at Ephesians chapter 4: 4-6: *There is one body, and one Spirit, just as you were called in one hope of your calling; one Lord, one faith, one baptism, one God and Father of all, Who is over all, and through all, and in you all.*

"Contemplating these and other New Testament verses I began to identify who we were in God. Having received Christ as our Saviour, we were birthed into *one* body, Christ's church: the church in our locality and the church across the world. United by *one* Spirit, God's Holy Spirit, who dwells in each member of Christ's body, God was enlivening and filling us that we might, under His direction, live and act in obedience to His word.

"He had given us *one* hope, sure and certain that anchors us in the promise that we will be eternally with Him in heaven. Submitting ourselves to *one* Lord, the world's only redeemer, we were saved by faith, that *one* faith gifted to us by God himself. Through acceptance and identification with Christ's death and the symbolic act of water baptism, we entered *one* baptism, which declares our allegiance to God, having received the covenant of His grace through the washing of regeneration so that we might walk in newness of life. Acknowledging that our *one* God is Father of all, who rules over us and presides over all.

"Essentially, these verses became the pillars which formed us as a body of God's people, the church in our locality at Rora.

"One Sunday morning Jim and I asked the church whether they felt we were worthy of the role of elders. Although Jim was older than me, we were both novices who humbly wanted to serve. The fellowship unanimously accepted us, and with the laying on of hands, set us apart as elders.

"Around the same time we took delivery of the hut we'd brought for five pounds off the Red Cross eighteen months earlier. Being the sort of man that I am," Malcolm said, with a nod of his head, "I decided to clear the old rose garden and erect the hut on the site.

"A short time later I got a telephone call from someone in the Dartmoor National Park's office in Bovey Tracey asking me to come to their office. I went and met a nice gentleman who proceeded to question me." Malcolm smiled. "I remember that conversation well.

"'Mr Ford,' he said. 'I understand you've put up a building without planning permission.'

"'Oh... yes,' I replied.

"'Do you know that you can't do that?'

"'I didn't.'

"'Please take the building down.'

"'No, I am not going to,' I said. 'It's for our youth work.'

"He scratched his head. 'You won't take it down?'

"'No!'

"'Will you get an architect's drawing then?'

"'No,' I repeated. 'I only paid five pounds for the hut.'

"He was at a bit of a loss for words. 'Well,' he said, finally. 'Have you got someone in your organisation who could do a square plan?'

"'What exactly is a square plan?' I asked.

"'It gives the basic design, measurements, position of the building in relation to other buildings, and the distance from your boundaries.'

"'Oh yes, we can do that,' I said, knowing that we didn't really have the money for such an expense. But Chrissie Cornish, who'd been with us from our earliest days at Ilsington Methodist Chapel, did a nice drawing which we sent in. They didn't give us planning permission exactly, instead they gave us a ten-year renewable license to use the building.

"I'm not a natural rebel. But I do tend to stand firm on what I believe to be right. I felt that the hut should be where it was, and I wasn't going to back down," said Malcolm, shrugging his shoulders. "It's a simple as that, maid. Not that we had any idea how it would be used."

Delivery of the hut, which was the registered
place of worship at Rora for over 40 years

Joe building the baptistry in the hut

"The number of visitors continued to grow. Sometimes we had too many guests for the number of rooms,
which was largely my fault, as I said yes to every inquiry
from those who wanted to come and stay. Christine took
that job off me and proceeded to organise the diary
much better than I could. Many missionaries stayed,
including our old friends Robin and Celia Talbot. They
were our first overseas contacts and they always came
and spent part of their furlough with us before they

returned to serve the Khmer of Thailand. We had lots of visiting speakers too. We tried to timetable them but, in the end we decided to allow them to come as they sensed God was leading them.

Robin and Celia Talbot and family - returning from the mission field

"On the seventh of November 1969, my birthday, God gifted us with another daughter. When Christine came home from hospital with the new baby, John Williams, who lived at on the edge of Stormsdown near Higher Whiddon, asked Christine what name we'd given our daughter. 'Anna,' Christine replied. Hearing this, John said, 'That's an appropriate name for these days. Like the Bible prophetess Anna who, serving in the temple, saw the coming of the Messiah, this child too may live to see the coming of the Lord.'

The five Ford children with baby Anna

"I'd been doing a few odd jobs for local farmers, milking herds when someone was ill or on holiday and doing gardening jobs as requested. As the work at Rora increased, I had to stop doing these odd jobs. The house, as I mentioned earlier, was structurally sound, although many rooms needed redecorating. The fellowship eagerly pitched in to help us, but there was still lots to do.

"People who came for holidays made donations. At first it was just a five-pound note or ten, then it started increasing. I'd already set up a bank account for monies that were coming into the fellowship and the house to keep them separate from our personal funds. However, someone pointed out that because the house was in my name and as I was registered self-employed, all monies that came into either the fellowship or the house would be counted as my income.

"Then, one day I was in Newton Abbot walking to the bank to pay in some money. I had the notes in my hand. It was a fair bit, perhaps a hundred or a hundred and twenty pounds. I opened my hand to look at the money and a voice spoke to me. 'That's my money not yours,' it said. I simply replied, 'Thank you, Lord.'

"I went home and talked to Jim Rowley and then went to see Mr Mitchelmore, the solicitor in Newton Abbot, who'd given us the private loan to buy Rora, to see whether what I'd been told was correct or not. He indicated that it was. The Inland Revenue would view all monies gifted to Rora as income to me. I asked him what we could do? He suggested we form a trust and register as a charity. I asked him to go ahead and do that, which he did, working out all the details with the charity commission. Apart from signing official documents, I did nothing. By July 1970 Rora House was no longer ours. It had become the Rora Christian Fellowship Trust.

"In truth, Rora House was never ours. I had only contributed twenty-six percent of the cost of the purchase, and the donations were paying the interest on the mortgage. Rora was, and always has been, the Lord's, although we weren't fully conscious of that at the time. Only as the work progressed did we realise that it belonged to Him.

"One of the first entries in the trustee's book, which of course began that year, reads sixteen pounds, fifteen shillings and tuppence in credit. Not much perhaps, but gifts had exceeded our expenditure. Hallelujah! What a faithful Saviour we have."

The Ford family, 1969

The Ford family, 1970

# 8

# And kindly help each other on

The lane that winds the half mile or so to Rora House has always been a rutted and potholed track. Belonging to the old farm next door, it's legally the neighbour's responsibility to maintain. When Malcolm and Christine purchased Rora House, they signed a contract with their neighbours, agreeing to contribute ten pounds per year towards the lane's upkeep.

"Sadly, however, our neighbour Mr McIlroy was slow to carry out repairs or improve drainage," said Malcolm. "The neighbour ran a riding school, and we had a steady stream of visitors. With the increased traffic the lane rapidly fell into disrepair. Something had to be done; and we agreed to put our annual ten-pound payment straight onto the lane. From that point onwards we poured gravel and tarmac into the potholes and kept the drainage channels unblocked. I think we've long exceeded our promised annual commitment.

· · ·

"WE WERE BECOMING a bit of a holiday destination for Christians across the country. Mr North and Norman Meeten had itinerant preaching ministries that took them north, south, east and west to newly forming fellowship groups. Through their travels links began to grow. Not that there was any formal connection; Mr North had no plans to start a denomination, but we simply enjoyed the familiar bond of fellowship in Christ.

"Liverpool, Exeter and Reading were just a few places where these fellowship groups, or house churches as they came to be known, were flourishing. Folk came for holidays, and the number of conferences we were hosting was also increasing. We added two further conferences to the calendar: one at the end of May, and one in September. The Liverpool fellowship also requested the use of the house for a men's weekend.

"After one conference in August, at which Mr North was our speaker, Gordon Harvey began a boys' camp. Pitching two or three old army tents on the lawn, Gordon gathered a couple of volunteers around him, and together they led the boys in a week of adventures and Bible studies. That camp proved extremely popular.

One of the first Boys' Camps

"Christine, as usual, carried the practical responsibility of organising food and accommodation for all the visitors and guests. With our five children to care for it was a mammoth task. The children pitched in as did the fellowship but it was clear we needed more help. Margie, who'd come to our farm with Gordon Harvey, felt the Lord calling her to give up her job and join us. Margie's mum wasn't a Christian and feared she might lose her daughter, but of course that never happened.

"Besides ourselves, Margie was our first full-time worker. She was twenty-two when she came to live in the house. Margie immediately rolled up her sleeves and got stuck in. There was a constant flow of people coming in and out of the front door. Margie helped Christine with the cleaning and washing. Together they cooked the meals for conference guests on the old Aga and ferried them out to visitors who initially sat at trestle tables set up in the covered terrace.

"During the conferences we served lunch and dinner. The number of people attending meant that we could no longer accommodate everyone in the lounge and so we had moved the meetings to our five-pound Red Cross hut. After each meeting the hut was cleared of canvas chairs to make room for trestle tables that became our temporary dining room. Again, the food was all ferried down from the kitchen, which was a bit of a lengthy process. We had little proper crockery but plenty of plastic cups and plates. It was all pretty spartan but no one minded. The young men of the fellowship would collect all the dirty dishes in large orange bowls, which is one of those odd images that sticks in your mind. They'd then return them to the kitchen ready for the team of washer-uppers, amongst whom there was always a great deal of mischief and hilarity.

Eating outside during conferences

"Joe and Beryl Maltby were frequent visitors and a tremendous help at conferences. We'd first met them when they accompanied Bob Love to Higher Whiddon, when we were beginning the negotiations to purchase Rora. They were both exactly ten years older than the two of us."

Joe & Beryl Maltby

Joe and Beryl came to know the Lord when Joe, who was working as a plastics engineer in Nottingham, accepted a job offer in Mumbai, India. Joe travelled ahead to start work and find a place for them to live as a family. Two months later Beryl and their two children, Sue eleven and Ricky four, followed, sailing as passengers on a cargo ship bound for India. There were just nine other passengers on the ship and the journey took one month. For Sue it was a great adventure, although her younger brother didn't quite feel the same.

It was while the family were in India that an American missionary couple shared the gospel with Joe and Beryl. Receiving the truth of God's transforming love turned their lives completely upside-down.

Even though Beryl had made a home for the family in Mumbai, Joe struggled to adjust to the hot, humid climate, plus the job wasn't what he'd hoped it would be. After two years Joe's boss offered to pay for his return passage to England. The company, Griflex, reinstated Joe to his former position, although the company had since moved from Nottingham to Leicester.

Settling in Leicester the family initially worshipped at their local Anglican church where Joe and Sue became bell-ringers, and Joe fulfilled his weekly commitment of winding the clock on the church tower. Later they joined a Church of Christ congregation, a small non-denominational autonomous church that met in Leicester. It was while they were involved with the Churches of Christ that they met Mr North and started a meeting in their own home.

In 1970 the company Joe worked for moved again, this time to Wales. Joe, Beryl, and Ricky moved to Llandegla; Sue was already married at this point.

"Yes," Malcolm continued. "Joe was a very gifted man and very capable. Despite several moves, the company he worked for kept his job open. He was obviously incredibly good at what he did.

"Uncle Joe usually wore a serious face, and to begin with it was difficult to gauge what he was thinking. But behind that sober face lurked an amazingly droll sense of humour. He told jokes without ever cracking a smile. Beryl was the complete opposite to her husband, a tiny, chatty powerhouse of a lady, who made up for Joe's quietness.

"We visited them when they were in Wales for a holiday. Their cottage was beautiful and set in the hills. But it was obvious they were seeking opportunities to serve the Lord, and, knowing me, I probably invited them to join us at Rora. Of course, you can't force anything like that on anyone, people must make their own decisions and know what God is calling them too.

"But God *was* moving. Mr North had spoken to them, suggesting that Rora might be a good fit. Sensing God was asking them to join us, Joe gave up his job, and they sold their lovely Welsh cottage. God also gave Joe a word regarding his role at Rora: *And his (Jonathan's) armour bearer said to him, 'Do all that is in your heart. Go then; here I am with you, according to your heart.'*[1] Joe felt that he should be my armour bearer. He did not come to Rora to lead as such, but to serve. Beryl felt that God was asking her to be a helpmeet to Christine.

"Simply, and without any fuss, they did what God had asked of them, and on the last day of September 1971 they moved to Rora with their son Ricky. Their arrival was an answer to our prayers; the growing ministry needed another married couple – a couple who could share in the practical aspects of the work and aid in the growth and maturing of the fellowship.

They gave their all. Yes," said Malcolm, "they laid down their lives for the vision God had given us at Rora.

"Even though the work was expanding, we had no blueprint for the way forward and constantly needed to seek the Lord's guidance. Wanting Him to equip us for the unfolding ministry, we used to spend much time in prayer and fasting. Aware that unless we knew and understood Him better, we, the fellowship, or the ministry, could not truly bear fruit.

"During the summer of that year we experienced problems with our water supply. Two natural springs coming off the moor supplied the house, but they were inadequate for the increased demand. One of the young people staying in the house, Phil Partridge, used a digger to dig out the mile-long trench that would make it possible for us to be connected to the mains water at Halford Cross.

"Requests to stay or use the house for conferences were overwhelming us. We had to turn people away as there just wasn't room enough to accommodate them. We had been praying and asking God to show us the next step, and here it was, opening out before us: We were to extend the premises. Jim and I discussed the possibilities, and after much deliberation agreed that I would approach the local Rural District Council with a large plan for expansion.

"I sensed I should demolish the old coach house and hayloft just beyond the front door of the house. Both buildings were already derelict, and in their place construct a three-storey building that would stand a little forward of the main house. It would be similar in style to Rora, with three floors. The ground floor would be a large dining room, kitchen, laundry and boot shed, while the other two would be bedrooms.

"It was September 1972 when I visited the planning office in Newton Abbot. I had a simple block plan with me and laid our petition before the planning officer.

"'It's too big, Mr Ford,' the planning officer said. 'We are willing to give you permission to demolish the outbuildings and replace them with a bungalow of equal size in the same style as the main house.'

"'That's not big enough for what I want,' I said. 'I'm not just looking for an extra couple of bedrooms, I'm after something much larger.' Of course, much larger in my mind meant a small type of conference centre.

"Permission denied, I returned to Rora and spoke again with Jim. We decided to continue pressing the authorities but resolved to contact an architect to get our requirements officially drawn up to submit to the planning office.

"In the meantime I bulldozed out the entire area beside the front door to the back of the house and up to our neighbour's fifteen-feet ancient lights[2] boundary. I moved all the soil down to the quarry on the edge of the woods, which created a huge mound of earth. Of course," said Malcolm with a cheeky grin, "I didn't have official permission to do that.

"The following year we made our second application. However, this time the man from the planning office wanted to come out and have a look at our premises and our proposed building's location. We arranged for him to come one Thursday. Not that he was coming alone, he was bringing a crowd with him. Some from Newton Abbot Urban planning office, some from Dartmoor National Park; a couple from Devon County, and our architect, John White.

"Now," said Malcolm. "Before we go any further, I must say that in all these projects I've always sensed the presence of the Lord close by, and I've always received a word of scripture, or prophecy confirming the way forward.

"The Wednesday evening before that particular Thursday we gathered for the prayer meeting and as was our normal practice we shared all our needs. I'd already been encouraging the fellowship to pray, but we naturally prayed for the planned meeting the following morning.

"One sister from the Exeter fellowship was there; she wasn't a regular member of our fellowship and she didn't know our exact circumstances, other than we were bursting at the seams. Anyway, she spoke out a prophetic word: *'Enlarge the place of your tent, and let them stretch out the curtains of your dwellings; do not spare; lengthen your cords and strengthen your stakes. For you will expand to the right and to the left.'*[3]

"In truth, that word didn't really mean much to me. But because we were praying specifically about the following day's meeting I took it as a word of confirmation from the Lord.

"Come Thursday, twelve planners and surveyors arrived at Rora's front door. Standing on the drive near the house they inspected the flattened garden and empty space where the coach house and stables had been. The planning officer asked me what I'd done.

"'I cleared the area,' I replied. 'Those outbuildings were dangerous.'

"The planning officer sighed. 'Your plans are still too

ambitious.' Then without so much as a walk around the premises, he continued, 'This is our proposal: remove the ground floor, making your extension on the west side just two stories high. Position your extension one metre back from the front of the house so that the new building doesn't overshadow the main house and it remains prominent. Site what would have been your ground floor dining room on the east side of the main house with four bedrooms above the new kitchen. And we will give you permission to use the large space behind the house to build a laundry and boot shed on the ground floor and a link corridor with space for three rooms on the first floor.'

"The scripture from Isaiah which the sister from Exeter had prophesied said, '... *for you will expand to the right and to the left...*'

"By the end of October 1973 we had planning permission. God had been faithful to His spoken word."

Mr & Mrs North singing in the hut during a
conference

# 9

# Regions Overseas, Regions Around

"A young man called Bob, who'd come to the Lord through a boy's club run by Steve Ward from Willand near Tiverton, felt God was calling him to join us in the practical ministry of the house at Rora. Vee, from Teignmouth, also felt the same. Together with Margie they were committed to making Rora a home that extended a warm welcome to all our visitors, whether they came for a day, a week or a month.

"Joe and Beryl, or Uncle Joe and Auntie Beryl as they were affectionately known by the young people, quickly found their niche. Auntie Beryl diligently ensured that all the house's laundry was washed and ironed, and that the rooms were clean and ready for visitors. Uncle Joe, an intensely practical man, was always ready to do anything I asked. He never forced his opinion on me but was ready with wise counsel and advice. They were faithful servants," said Malcolm with a distant look in his eye.

"Those who were specifically called to work practically in the house had to trust the Lord for their needs.

We supplied them with a room and fed them but they had to trust the Lord for everything else. Some had a part-time job whilst others did not.

"Folk like Mike Coles and Chris French lived with us but had full-time jobs outside. They contributed towards their bed and board. While others, like Peter Russek, a German travelling in France, just turned up on our doorstep. Having met Jim and Molly while they were on holiday in France they'd promptly given Peter an invitation to Rora. Peter came for a few months and was a great member of the team. He built a wall down the side of the drive which is still standing. He left and married Anne, an English girl, and they returned to Germany.

"Many fellowship members also helped. Some regularly did the ironing or cleaned bathrooms, whilst others baked so that our freezers were well stocked ready to feed our guests." Malcolm sighed. "Our enthusiasm for God brought a unity of heart and spirit. Everyone was involved and committed to the practical tasks which enabled the ministry of God's Word to grow.

"We were a church, but really, we were a family. Rora was a home. Initially, we ate all our meals together, and we'd often spend the evenings sitting in the breakfast room off the kitchen − it was the one room with an open fire. We'd read or chat while the ladies would knit or sew.

"People used to come and ask us about running a community, or, conversely, they wanted to give us advice about how to run a community. It was the 1970s when community life was popular and people were interested in living, working, and fellowshipping together. They felt it was a new move in the life of the church that needed to be embraced and developed. But we had no such preconceived ideas or plan.

"Some communities emphasised the authority of the leader, intimating that he should be the one to make decisions for families and their children under his care, but I never agreed with that position. In fact, I remember the Lord speaking to me, telling me that each person or family needed to be independent. We had no desire to control anyone, particularly later as some of the couples started having children. The father and mother were to parent their own children.

"The number of missionaries who stayed with us grew steadily and it was through their stories and testimonies that we learned about people in other lands who'd never heard the name of Jesus before. We'd always been interested in the work of God beyond our locality, and, as I mentioned before, the verse in Acts chapter 1 was a key verse: *'You shall be witnesses to me in Jerusalem and in all Judea and Samaria, and to the ends of the earth.'*

"In fact, I find the book of Acts deeply inspiring. It's about God and the actions of the apostles. To my mind the church is the place of God's activities. Taking the gospel, the good news about Jesus Christ out into the world, whether that's in your village, town, city or county and beyond, should be a part of the church's DNA because God has mission on His heart.

"To listen to those who've gone beyond their own borders and experienced our God working in a foreign culture and context is inspiring. It is like reading the book of Acts all over again. I remember one elderly gentleman coming to the church. His name was Willie Burton."

Born into a privileged home, Willie Burton's mother was an English aristocrat and his father a ship's captain. Willie himself was an accomplished sportsman as well as an acclaimed artist. After becoming a Christian at college, he turned his back on his privileged lifestyle and entered full-time Christian ministry. As an engineer, Willie used all his skills for the sake of the gospel in the Congo.

"He was a stout, larger-than-life character," said Malcolm. "He always used to have props to illustrate the message he was seeking to communicate. You couldn't turn a blind eye to him or his message. The second time he came to visit us, he'd just buried his wife out in the Congolese jungle. Despite his sorrow, Jesus shone through him.

"Anyway, he took a chair and sat in the middle of Rora lounge; it was before we moved our meetings to the hut. He asked for a dustpan and brush. We were somewhat surprised but nevertheless supplied him with the dustpan and brush. He proceeded to brush the floor, telling us that we had to clear all the mess of sin out of lives. He didn't just say it, he demonstrated it which added impact to his message.

"If you're a pastor or a leader, you must exalt the church to the work of God beyond your home, beyond your borders even. There's always work to do on our doorstep but as John Wesley so rightly said, 'The world is my parish.'

"THE FELLOWSHIP WAS GROWING STEADILY, and naturally romance blossomed amongst many of the young people. Gordon Harvey and Chrissie Cornish married. We had no registration for marriages, so marriages were conducted elsewhere. Gordon and Chrissie were married in the Methodist Church in Newton Abbot. A few months later Mike Coles and Faith Warren got married at St James, Teignmouth.

"Chris and Val and others quickly followed. However, instead of marrying in a denominational church they decided to marry at Rora. This was not an easy choice. We had come out of the established church and weren't able to conduct marriages at Rora. Some got married at the Registry Office in Newton Abbot and then had a simple ceremony in the lounge at Rora. It was neither grand nor formal. Understandably, many parents were displeased. This turned out to be an exacting time for several of the young people as they had to make their case for marrying at Rora. Some parents were quite forceful in their opinions. I can understand their frustrations. Married in a registry office and then conducting a white wedding in Rora's big lounge the same afternoon, it must have seemed a world away from a traditional church wedding and smart reception. But back then, we were crossing cultural norms.

"A PATTERN WAS BEGINNING to form with conferences at Easter, Whitsun and during the summer and then the last week of October. Of course, there was lots going on in between too.

"Then one conference, I think it was Whitsun (now called Spring Bank holiday) because Mr North was always our speaker at Whitsun – anyway, Mr North came over to me in the tea break and whispered that

Len and Iris Moules would be visiting as they were on holiday in Bovey Tracey, a few miles away. They were staying with Brian Roseveare, cousin of Doctor Helen Roseveare who'd been a medical missionary in the Congo.

Len & Iris Moules with Mr & Mrs North on
Rora terrace

"Themselves former missionaries to the Bhotiya people in the High Himalaya on the edge of Tibet, Len and Iris had returned to England in 1961. Since then, Len had been both the UK and International Director of WEC. Mr North had spoken at WEC headquarters which some people found surprising, and he'd invited Len and Iris over to Rora. They arrived one evening when the hut was absolutely packed. In contrast to today, when you might get twenty or thirty at our conferences, then there'd be at least a *hundred* and thirty, or perhaps even two hundred. Len and Iris came in discreetly, sitting themselves in one corner at the back of the hut. Mr North introduced us to them and that was the beginning of an inspiring friendship," said Malcolm.

"The link with WEC flourished, and we always seemed to have a few WEC missionaries attending our conferences. On one occasion, Christine severely burned her hands whilst preparing dinner. A missionary family, who were attending the conference, invited the two of us to stay at Bulstrode, the then headquarters of WEC.

"Christine couldn't do much else other than rest, and so we took them up on their invitation. She accompanied the family to Bulstrode and I followed a few days later.

"Located just outside Gerrards Cross in Buckinghamshire, Bulstrode is off the A40 Oxford Road. Turning into WEC's entrance that first time, I reached the end of their drive to find a rambling red brick building before me. With its impressive tower perched above the front entrance it certainly looked imposing. Len had bought the mansion for WEC from the Bruderhof, a German Anabaptist Christian movement. The property had been in an almost derelict state and WEC was slowly renovating it. We subsequently visited Bulstrode many times.

"Len was an amazing man. Gifted in so many areas and with a great capacity for work. He also had great vision. He loved mountain climbing and enjoyed climbing in the High Himalayas. I think Len saw the Christian faith as a constant climb closer to God.

"He was also a great encouragement to me, giving me sound advice and directions on how to establish the church more firmly. I've got it all here," said Malcolm patting his big brown file. "Len wrote everything down in his meticulous hand. He gave me clear instructions on how to work with a board of trustees and helped me consider how to develop the ministry. He was a visionary and he told me that all visionary leaders need to be thinking ahead, that they must be seeking the Lord for His plans for the next five years so that they can lead those under their care. I'd never thought about anything like that before.

"We also learned a lot by watching the way Bulstrode operated practically too. The place was huge, and those who ran the headquarters, or those missionaries who were home on furlough, all lived very simply. Each had their own room or small apartment type of thing. They ate their meals together, and each one trusted the Lord for their finances. It was a confirmation to me regarding the ministry at Rora as we had established it along remarkably similar lines.

"One Sunday afternoon we were standing in the hall at Rora. Len and Iris were just leaving and I said, 'Len, give me an acronym for RORA.' Without a moment's hesitation he answered, Regions Overseas, Regions Around.' That was it. The phrase sums up the heart of the vision and concept of Rora, and it stuck.

"WITH THE IMMINENT addition of further accommodation we desperately needed to increase our water supply. Even though we had a connection to the mains supply at Halford Cross, we rarely used it as it was expensive and we preferred to use the springs near us if we could. We'd already replaced the rusty pipes up to our reservoir and renewed our agreement with our neighbour, but it wasn't enough. Thankfully, we were able to tap into an additional spring which we merged with our original supply. With a gift we'd bought all the parts we needed and did most of the work ourselves.

"Thinking about the growing ministry and the building projects that lay ahead I approached our neighbour about buying some of his land. There had been the option to purchase some acres when we first bought Rora, but we hadn't thought about it then. However, as the ministry was expanding, it seemed worth asking. Our neighbour's blunt 'no' answered my question. I just shrugged my shoulders and thought nothing further.

"Less than six months later our neighbour turned up at our kitchen door to ask me whether I was still interested in buying fifteen and a half acres, that was the three fields adjoining the lane. He was offering these fifteen and a half acres for ten thousand pounds which would bring us up to twenty-two acres in total. We immediately shared this with the church and prayed. As a fellowship we agreed to buy the land. A kind gift enabled us to pay off the outstanding mortgage on the house, and we received a wonderful gift of four thousand pounds from missionary friends towards the purchase of the land. We took out a mortgage for the other six thousand pounds, and by February 1974 the land became Rora's.

"We also had gifts in the bank earmarked for stage one of the extensions. With the growth of the work, Jim Rowley and I asked Uncle Joe to consider becoming a trustee, which he did. He officially took up his position as treasurer/secretary on the seventeenth of August 1974.

"Ready to start the building work, we called the builders. The shell went up quickly and by early October 1974 the boot-shed, laundry, and the first-floor link corridor for the proposed extension of the main house to the west wing were completed. With a little money in the bank we resolved to step out and begin stage two: the new kitchen, dining room and four bedrooms that would come off the east side of the house.

"We had much enthusiasm as the builders began the work. The footings dug, blocks were laid up to damp proof course level, and then in January 1975 the money started to dry up and the whole project ground to a halt."

Ford family, 1971

Building Phase 1

# 10

# Brick upon brick. Faith – a bag of cement

"We owed the builder who'd put in the footings and taken us to damp proof course about twelve hundred pounds. We resolved to pay him off and then wait, imagining that the finances for the extension would soon start trickling in again. But no further money came in. One year passed. We didn't add a single brick or block to stage two. Our visitors were gracious and affirming. However, during the second and third years some started making flippant remarks, calling the proposed extension my 'white elephant'. I held on in faith, knowing that God had spoken to me, telling people that it was God's will and that He would bring the building work to completion in His time.

"Despite my supposed 'white elephant', the fellowship continued growing. The vibrancy of the church was drawing new people. Many families joined us, or upped sticks and moved to Devon to be a part of the fellowship. Jack and Jill Frost were one. Both Jack and Jill clearly felt God called them to Rora. Jack gave up his highly respectable job as a government inspector of x-ray equipment in London to move to Liverton, although their move was far from straightforward. Their house in Kings Langley didn't sell easily, and Jack's job in Torquay, along with their eldest two children's schooling, started before their house sold. For several months Jack and his two eldest children Ruth and Steve lived with us at Rora until they were finally able to move into a large house in the village called Moorlands.

Jack and Jill Frost

"With their five children Jack and Jill became a vital part of the fellowship. As an engineer of x-ray equipment Jack was very practical and enthusiastically volunteered to help in whatever way he could. Jack and Jill's home was always open. They had a mobile home in their garden, which during conferences was full. It wasn't unusual to have twenty or more crowded into their tiny kitchen. Very often on a Sunday, after the fellowship lunch, we'd find our way to their place for tea. Jill was an excellent cook and her Victoria sandwich tasted divine. I remember we had a yearly tradition going – we'd celebrate Christmas Day at Rora, followed by Boxing Day at the Frosts.

Jack & Malcolm (in latter years)

"Not only was the church flourishing but visitors flowed in and out of Rora. Boys' Camp, now led by Gren and Steve Peters and Steve Ward from the Tiverton fellowship, was thriving. Christine and two other sisters decided it was time to start a camp for the girls, which we simply called Girls' Houseparty. The first few took place at Instow, a North Devon village on the estuary of the River Taw and Torridge. Peggy and Iris, two friends of ours, had a house there and invited Christine to use it for Girls' Houseparty; I think thirteen girls attended that first houseparty.

"Chris and Shirley French left Rora to establish a work in Newton Abbot. Chris was a born evangelist and eager to share the gospel with anyone who came across his path. Mike and Faith Coles joined Chris and Shirley and Uncle Joe, and our Jeremy took on the running of the small bookstall we had started at Rora."

Malcolm laughed. "We also had a little shop running, selling things visitors might need. I had the idea of buying food and selling it to the fellowship at a bit of profit so that we could make a little money to put into the trust. I didn't realise that a charitable trust couldn't have business dealings. Our solicitor advised us to buy a pre-registered company off the shelf, so to speak, which is what I did. For years we ran the shop and bookstall through that company and put the profits into the trust. Mind you, my idea of selling food to the fellowship was one of those that didn't work out. It might have seemed like a good idea at the time, but it wasn't really God ordained.

"As our children grew up we started caring for other children too. Initially we had children from the youth club we'd worked with who were experiencing difficulties at home or whose parents felt overwhelmed. With the parents' permission, children came to us for temporary shelter and care.

"Somehow or other the lady responsible for children's foster care at Devon County Council heard what we were doing and asked whether we'd be willing to register as foster parents. We signed all the forms and for about three or four years cared for fourteen or so teenaged children.

"With our children attending the village Church of England school we also became heavily involved in the life of the school and the village. Of course, the village was a lot smaller then, and the community much more closely-knit. The school had about eighty children, whereas it has over three hundred today.

"We were both on the Parent Teacher Association, and Christine ran the pre-school group for more than twenty years. Initially our children, along with our neighbour's children, walked the mile and half to school, but eventually we got a minibus to take them back and forth. The school and parents then asked us whether we'd be willing to go around the village picking up and dropping off other school children which of course we were.

"Chris Stoneman, who was living in the house, or one of the other lads would be their driver. There were no seat belts back then, and they just piled into the bus and Chris would tell them about the Lord. We were running youth work in the village hall and so everyone knew us. That came to a natural end when our children left the school, and the rules for driving buses and children around began to change.

"They were full days," Malcolm said with a sigh. "The hut, although we started referring to it as the meeting hall, was solemnised for dedications, marriages, and funerals. Uncle Joe was the registrar which meant we were free to conduct weddings, funerals, and so forth.

"Once or twice a month, I can't quite remember how often it was, I'd join five or six other Christian brothers; they were mainly from Brethren assemblies, and we'd visit a village in the area. Standing on a corner, we sang, shared testimonies and preached the gospel. People rarely came out, but they'd have their doors and windows open so that they could hear. George Santer, who'd come to Julian's thanksgiving service at Rora a few years earlier, often accompanied us. He would play his old pedal organ or the accordion. They were precious times."

Yet they were tough years too. The trustees' book recorded each year as difficult financially. Rora was barely able to cover their bank charges, let alone reduce their loan or relieve their debts at the bank. Harsh inflation, which in the 1970s was running extremely high, with the rate peaking at over twenty-four percent in 1975, coupled with a drop in income, made it impossible for the fellowship to meet all their payments.

"We held onto the Lord and continued in prayer, not knowing how we were going to make ends meet but trusting that He would guide us through. We set our financial position before the church and invited all who sensed that they should contribute to do so. We wanted to reduce our debt. Even though we weren't a wealthy fellowship, many gave generously, and we managed to meet the interest payments. But we were not able to recommence building work.

"The three fields we'd bought from our neighbour were bringing in some income from the twice-yearly sale of hay, and we used these funds to pay off the mortgage we had on the land.

"Some of us began to wonder whether we'd departed from the Lord's principles in borrowing finances for the building projects and the land. We repented and rededicated our lives to Him and the vision and purposes He'd given us. As we waited, we understood more clearly – we had simply assumed that God would supply the money we needed for the building work as He had already done. We had not had a specific word from Him to proceed. We acknowledged that we had rushed on ahead.

"We also began to realise that there was some disunity in the fellowship. We weren't all fully submitted to God. Together we acknowledged our disobedience and repented. In March 1976 we set aside Wednesday lunch times for prayer and fasting. We sensed God wanted to draw us closer to Himself, and we did not want to miss that.

"Jim Rowley, who'd been with us from the farm days, resigned as a trust board member. He wasn't completely happy with the management of the trust; he felt that we were moving along a business line. For conscience's sake, and in fairness to the other trustees, he felt he should resign. Evidently this was a painful and difficult decision, not made in haste but after much prayer and heart-searching. With regret, we accepted his resignation. There was no friction or animosity between us, and Jim and Molly continued attending the fellowship.

"Despite the challenges, we had all we needed for each day and we were learning valuable lessons. As a body we were learning to ask the Lord to supply each need as it came, which He did.

"There was one time," said Malcolm, raising his eyebrows, "when we hadn't been able to pay the quarterly electricity bill. I think it was about sixty pounds. The man from the South West Electricity board was due to arrive that day to disconnect us from the mains supply. At morning prayers, those of us in the house agreed to put a basket out on the kitchen table. At coffee time, which was ten thirty, I checked to see whether there was anything in the basket. Now there are three doors into the kitchen, which is now the playroom – one external and two internal.

"When I returned, I saw the basket piled high with old one-pound notes. I counted them out; there were exactly sixty. Being a nosey sort of fellow I began asking those who lived in the house if they'd seen anyone enter or exit the kitchen. Everyone shook their head; no one had seen anyone.

"The man from the electricity board arrived. I told him I had the sixty pounds, which of course he couldn't take. I had to go down to Newton Abbot to pay the bill, and then the electricity board told the electrician not to cut us off.

JACK FROST BECAME a trustee in December 1977, and Malcolm started to sense that they should resume the building work. A line of scripture: 'precept upon precept, line upon line,' spoke to him of 'brick upon brick.'[1] Malcolm talked with Uncle Joe, telling him that he intended to share *the* word with the fellowship the following Sunday morning.

"The church listened, but no one responded," said Malcolm with a heavy sigh. "There wasn't even an 'Amen', which left me perplexed.

"'Brick upon brick.' The words refused to leave me. We went through Christmas and were getting back into the swing of work after the holidays. 'Brick upon brick,' it was still strong in me. I thought, oh dear I can't go on much longer with this phrase beating around my brain.

"I explained my position to Uncle Joe, telling him that I planned to speak with the fellowship on Sunday morning. Clearing my throat, I stood to share: 'In early December, I brought you a word I believed that God had given me,' I said. 'That word has not left me. I believe that it refers to stage two of our building project. As you know, we are up to damp proof course and have been at that level for three years now. Together, we have acknowledged our disobedience to the Lord and sought

His forgiveness. 'Brick upon brick,' is the word. We still have no money, but there is nine inches of soil that needs to be dug out so that the chippings and the concrete floor can be laid. So, for those of you who believe that this word is from the Lord, I am inviting you to assemble at the site next Saturday morning wearing your wellington boots, bringing a spade or a wheelbarrow, and trusting the Lord with me. We'll dig in *faith*, knowing that He will supply all we need.'

"At the end of the meeting a brother, Roger Perring, came to me. He was a farmer who also did a bit of building work on the side. He had an account with the local builders' yard in Ashburton.

Roger and May

'When you need your first load of blocks,' he said to me, 'go down to the builders' merchant and put a load on my account.' Of course, we weren't ready for concrete blocks at that stage, but his generosity was an encouragement.

"In the evening meeting Uncle Joe quietly said that

he thought God was asking him to build, although he admitted with a slight smile that he'd never laid a block in a major building project before. He was sitting opposite me, and I jumped to my feet, went to him, and laying my hands on him prayed that the Lord would give him all the necessary skills he needed to complete the task.

"Come Saturday morning a crowd of men, all those who were able, came to dig. We dug out the nine inches, although in the far corner of the proposed building we needed a load of chippings to build up so that the foundation was level. Of course, we had no money to buy chippings, so the church prayed, and I decided to approach our neighbour to see whether we could scour his land for stones. He agreed. Easter weekend we had a group of young people from Liverpool staying with us. On the Saturday morning we took the Land Rover, trailer, and several buckets, one bucket between two I think it was, up onto our neighbour's land and started picking up stones. I told them: 'don't pick up anything bigger than an inch and a half,' which is what they did. We must have picked up a couple of tons of stones at least, but they did the job for the infill.

"I remember we reached the point where we needed to order our first load of concrete. Again, it was a Saturday morning. I was standing outside the library window near the front door waiting for the arrival of the concrete. I saw the lorry slowly trundling up the lane and watched as it turned into the drive and passed the magnolia tree at the bottom. I was standing with my hands behind my back. What no one knew was that I was ten pounds short on the payment for the concrete. Just before the lorry reached me, someone (I have no idea who), walked behind me and pressed something into my hand. Thinking it might be a telephone message or something like that, I looked at the piece of paper. It was a ten-pound note.

"When it came time to order our first load of blocks I went to the builders' merchants and put them on Roger's account as he'd instructed. Uncle Joe started the block work with a gentleman called Alan Marsden, a bachelor who used to attend conferences, who felt that the Lord had called him to work with Uncle Joe. Alan had some experience in the building industry. He was from London and had grown up in a Barnardo's Children's Home. When he started working with Uncle Joe he packed up his home and came to live with us at Rora. He was with us until he went to be with the Lord a few years ago.

"And so we proceeded, 'brick upon brick,' according to the word that the Lord had spoken to my heart, watching as God supplied every one of our needs. A few weren't comfortable with our programme of adding buildings to Rora, and they left quietly. There was no upset or disagreement, we simply held differing opinions. We are all different. Some focus wholly on the spiritual life of the church, while others emphasise the practical above all else. But I think there must be balance; we must root and centre ourselves in God first, and the fruit of that relationship will work out practically in the tasks He gives us to complete."

Conferences at Rora

# 11

# Incoming and outgoing...
# working together

"The building of stage two at Rora took nearly five years to complete. With dogged determination Uncle Joe and Alan Marsden continued laying blocks, positioning windows and rendering the outer walls. Often they'd run out of materials, and there'd be no money left in the kitty. We'd immediately gather, it didn't matter when it was, and we'd pray, bringing our requests to God. Every time, without fail, a gift would be handed to us or a cheque arrive in the post. Whether it was five pounds or two hundred, we received every gift with thankful hearts knowing that God was enabling us to continue; knowing that we could buy the next bag of cement, the next load of sand, or eighty concrete blocks. Sometimes a larger gift would come in and we'd be able to order a whole truckload of blocks.

"This was a time of simple trust in God where we saw countless answers to prayer. The fellowship gathered around us, supporting the work in every way they could. Our faith grew as we understood more deeply the bond of the body of Christ and our utter dependency on

God. Although this did not detract from the fact that the work involved hard physical labour. At least sixty tons of chippings and concrete were wheelbarrowed across the house's front terrace to the work site. On Saturdays, and some of the lighter summer evenings, members of the fellowship would come and help. God consistently sent us assistance at the right time.

"In the dining room we planned to have a large servery area between the kitchen and the dining area. To support the first-floor structure above the servery, a long, heavy concrete lintel, weighing in the region of one ton, needed raising to ceiling level. We had no funds to hire a crane, but we did have a group of young American Christians staying with us. We'd met the Americans at Bulstrode; they were part of a group called Christian Corp, started by an Irishman Ernest O'Neill who lived in America. On the Saturday morning the young Americans gathered at the building site, made a tower of blocks, and by dints of strength and sheer determination lifted the lintel into position.

"The whole fellowship laid the concrete floor while Jack Frost led the team that installed the electrics. For three-hundred pounds we purchased a second-hand cooker from a school in Wincanton for the kitchen. It was a monster of a thing but exceptionally reliable, and somehow or other we managed to transport it from the school to Rora using a trailer on the back of my car. It lasted us about twenty years.

"So," said Malcolm rubbing his hands together, "the building work advanced, 'brick upon brick.'

"Of course," he continued with a laugh, "we started using the building before it was finished, which drove Uncle Joe up the wall. He liked to finish a job completely before allowing us to step in and use it, but I've always been eager to get on and use what's available, and Uncle Joe was endlessly gracious.

"At the May conference in 1980, we had people sleeping on mattresses on the concrete floor of what would be the upstairs four bedrooms above the kitchen. The walls were just block work and there was no ceiling in place. In March 1981 our eldest son Stephen and his wife Caroline held their wedding reception in the still uncompleted dining room. Only one wall of the dining room had plaster on it, and we set the top table for the bride and groom in front of it so that it looked better for the photos. We covered the bare floor with old pieces of carpet.

Phase 2 Building - Kitchen & Dining Room

"George Santer, who we first met when we were involved in the distribution of the Free Christian newspaper *The Challenge,* had been coming along to conferences and meetings at Rora for several years. He was a friend of Julian, the young man killed in a motorbike accident shortly after we moved to Rora. George attended Julian's memorial service, although he later admitted that as a Brethren man himself he'd partly come to Julian's memorial to spy for the Brethren," Malcolm said with a laugh. "I guess they were trying to suss out whether we were okay or not.

"George, a bachelor from Totnes, was something of a spiritual gypsy.

George Santer

His family attended the Totnes Gospel Hall, but George was well known in most of the Gospel Halls in Devon. He played the piano, went to youth camps, and preached and taught in every gospel hall that was open to him. A respected Brethren man he was also seeking and searching for something more of God himself. He'd heard of the awakening and the working of the Holy Spirit in people's lives, and eager to experience that himself he'd invited God to work more deeply in his life.

"George was a shy, retiring type of fellow really, although when he shared God's truth he spoke with great passion and boldness. He sang beautifully and, untaught as a pianist, his playing lifted our spirits as we worshipped the Lord together.

"He moved to Rora and became our gardener, and he did small maintenance jobs too, whilst retaining his vagabond existence. He lived simply; his room was tiny, and he had few possessions. I think he spent all his money on stamps. Countless people whom he cared for and mentored received letters from him. At a moment's notice he'd pick up his battered old bag and be on his travels, visiting friends, encouraging them in God, and returning a few weeks later. We never really knew where he went. At Christmas he sent out greeting cards alongside a text for the coming year. In the year that he died he had five thousand cards prepared for posting.

"There are so many," Malcolm said with a sigh. "So many who came. So many who've been a part of the outworking of the vision and purposes of the church. Too many to mention in the pages of this book, but each one has contributed to the life and ministry of the fellowship and work at Rora.

"The Girls' Houseparty which started in Peg and Iris's home in Instow quickly outgrew that location. Through links with the school in Ashburton we were able to use facilities in the village of Stoke Fleming in South Devon. Mind you, it wasn't ideal, as the houseparty was held during the Easter holidays which were often cold and wet.

Peter and Ruth Elks

"Chris and Val, who'd been living in the house with us, sensed God calling them to India to be involved in mission work. In 1982 they travelled to Gorakhpur where they did nine months studying the local language before beginning an itinerate teaching ministry alongside an Indian brother called Jia. Likewise, Pete Elks, who was one of the young men living in the attic of the house, believed God was calling him to Southeast Asia. Pete had already started dating Jack and Jill's eldest daughter, Ruth. Their romance blossomed and they married in 1981. The church commissioned them as missionaries to Thailand shortly afterwards.

"Chris French, who had moved out of Rora with his wife Shirley to set up the fellowship in Newton Abbot, had some connection with Open Doors – an organisation started in 1955 by a young Dutch Christian called Brother Andrew. Moved by the curbed liberties of those living under the dictates of Soviet Communism, Brother Andrew sought to bring solace to Christians who felt lost to the rest of the world. Taking a suitcase of Bibles behind the curtain of walls, fences, and minefields,

Brother Andrew began a mission that continues to supply Bibles and biblical materials to those living in hostile regions of the world.

"Somehow the connection with Open Doors sparked a link with Jack and Jill's eldest son Steve, and his wife Linda. In the early 1980s, Steve and Linda started taking trips to Eastern Europe, and invited Christine to accompany them, ostensibly as grandmother to help care for their two small children.

"Christine came home from that first trip behind the Iron Curtain full of stories. In delivering Bibles and Christian materials, they'd begun to get a sense of the restrictions the people in the east lived under. Surveillance monitored people's movements, informers regularly reported any activities deemed contrary to the communist ideology, and Christians endured humiliation as the regime sought to discredit them and their faith in God. Many Christians' salaries were highly taxed leaving them on the edge of poverty, and many church leaders spent time in prison.

"It was evident that these people needed God's Word and Christian literature. But those living behind the Iron Curtain also needed strengthening in those dark days of persecution. They needed to know that the rest of the world had not forgotten them. Even though Christine had gone as a grandmother, it was obvious that God had called her to this new work." Malcolm shook his head. "As was often the case, the Lord used Christine to prompt me in my thinking. We were, after all, in the ministry together. Her commitment made me ask the question, 'Should I take a trip too?'

"Shortly after I asked this question Chris and Val in Gorakhpur requested that someone from the church visit them. I was aware that we also had Pete and Ruth in Thailand. In my heart I guess I knew that it was a part of the church's ministry of care, and in particular, part of the pastor's mandate to encourage and, when possible, visit members of the church serving in different locations. But I am a Devonian, and to my way of thinking Devon was one of the most beautiful places on earth, and naturally I had no desire to leave the county. Of course, God had to take that type of thinking out of my heart.

"We were a young fellowship then and not exactly sure how to proceed. Gathering the following Sunday evening after receiving Chris and Val's request, I brought the matter to the church and asked them to pray, instructing them that if anyone sensed God was calling them to go, then they should just pipe up. No sooner had we started to pray than I sensed the Lord saying to me, '"You've got to go."' *Dearie me*, I thought, I've never travelled before. I'm forty and I'd never even had a passport.

"I said to the fellowship, 'There's no need to pray anymore, the Lord has spoken to me. But please pray because it seems impossible to go as I don't have any money.' That's one of the things we used to do – we always shared our personal needs, and would lay hands on one another and pray that God would provide.

"We were meeting in the house lounge that evening, and a sister who was sitting on the window seat said, 'I have the money for your ticket.' It was seven hundred and fifty pounds. She signed the cheque there and then and I was able to visit each family for three weeks.

"It was the first time I'd left Britain. I knew a bit about India and its poverty, but to see affluence and poverty existing side by side was astonishing. It was chaotic and noisy with people and buildings crowded in every street. I stayed with Chris and Val, listening to their encouragements and struggles, and visiting their friends. Later I travelled with Norman Meeten to a conference in the northeast of the country, and then on to Pete and Ruth in Thailand. The conditions in Thailand were less basic, and it was good to spend time with Pete and Ruth. Those visits opened my eyes to a larger world in which God was at work. They also prepared me for the next step.

"One week after my return from Asia, Dave Medlock from the Reading fellowship approached me to ask whether I'd be willing to accompany him on a road trip to Poland, as his assistant driver was no longer able to go with him. *You don't need me*, I thought. *You're a rally driver, boy,* but I agreed anyway.

"It must have been April 1984. We travelled through Belgium and West Germany, staying overnight in a small bed-and-breakfast place before driving to the West-East German border. The town had a cobbled square, and I had this strong image of shiny black boots marching across the square which put me in mind of the Second World War. That strong image stuck with me. Leaving West Germany at the Helmstedt crossing, it was like we'd entered a different world. We had travelled just ten or fifteen metres down the road, and yet the difference was palpable, the contrast huge. Gone was the normal hustle and busyness of the town. Solemn faces replaced the laughter and chatter we'd just seen a short time ago. A few drably dressed people quietly walked the streets, avoiding our gaze. The temperature had not changed, but I felt a chill in my soul. *So, this is Communism.* I didn't cry, but I did feel deeply moved.

"We headed to the Polish border early in the morning. When we arrived at Frankfurt Oder, Dave instructed me to be quiet and let him do the talking, which I did. His large Citroen was loaded with stuff, which was all covered. We crossed the border without any trouble and continued our journey, travelling south beyond Warsaw to a town called Lodz where we were to join a young people's weekend.

"We drove through Lodz and travelled east down a long straight country road for about fifteen kilometres. A little way ahead I saw young people waving at us. Expecting us, they had spotted Dave's large foreign car, which naturally stood out against the Fiats and Warszawas. Dave suddenly turned right and pulled into a yard behind a largely derelict farm set in the forest where the young people's weekend was being held. As soon as we got out of the car the young people covered the vehicle with a tarpaulin. *Whatever is this*, I thought. *What's all this secrecy for?* I'd never experienced anything like it. It was too risky for us as westerners to stay at the farm overnight, so we stayed at a hotel and drove to the camp each day. Then I realised, this was no pleasure trip but something serious. Coming from the west, I only knew freedom. I'd never had to walk in the shadows, checking what was happening around me all the time.

"We had a good weekend with the young people and returned to England without incident. But the whole experience was unsettling, or, more accurately, it set me thinking. Here were people living behind this *curtain* in great poverty and oppression, longing for bread and sustenance. What could I do? I didn't have a word of scripture as such, as I normally do when starting a new work, but there were stirrings in my heart: '*Those who tend to the poor shall be blessed.*'

"Open Doors asked Christine whether she'd be willing to take another trip into Eastern Europe. Then I understood. More than physical poverty, there was a poverty of God's word; they used to refer to the Bible as Bread. This *Bread*, I could take to the believers in those locked countries. I took up the challenge and Christine and I started travelling together."

Bob and Marg Jones

Chris and Val Stoneman

# 12

# Delivery of Bread and the gathering of the beloved

Malcolm and Christine's children were growing up and leaving home, and God had called them to travel. They worked with Open Doors under the leadership of Alan Hall, travelling to Eastern Germany, Hungary, and the former Czechoslovakia and Yugoslavia. Driving their vehicle to Open Door's headquarters they would leave it in Holland and continue in another vehicle filled with materials which they would drive to its designated destination.

"Reaching the border of the country we were due to enter, we'd pray that we'd be granted entry," said Malcolm. "There were no embassies or consulates where you could get your visa in advance then. You simply had to trust that the border official would grant you passage. Amazingly, the guards never denied us a visa, although we did have to provide them with our complete itinerary. Those guards thoroughly searched our vehicles; well, maybe not that thoroughly," said Malcolm with a wink. "Those vehicles were marvellous;

they had all sorts of concealed spaces, and the border guards never discovered our treasure.

"We often travelled in a campervan or towed a caravan. Usually we stayed on camp sites, which we'd already detailed to the border guards. Each day we'd leave the site, travel to a designated location, perhaps in a forest, quarry, or along some deserted stretch of road, where we passed the materials to our appointed contact. The schedule was exacting and we tried to keep to the time, but we didn't always manage.

"Once, we were carrying a heavy load of eight hundred Bibles and sixty packs of materials for a teachers' conference, in a Renault van. The van was running close to the ground and refused to go above fifty miles an hour.

"Friends had warned us that we could experience problems if we arrived late at the border crossing and of course we were late, added to which, there was a lady border guard on duty – the women were supposedly tougher than the men. Thankfully, we experienced no difficulties. We entered the country and made our way to the home of the young pastor who was going to take delivery of the Bibles etc.

"Unfortunately we arrived in daylight, and the young pastor told us that we could do nothing until nightfall. The pastor and his wife kindly invited us into their home and we spent five hours chatting. When it was completely dark, the pastor told me to drive the vehicle into the church grounds, as they lived in the manse, and he would open the garage doors. I was to drive straight into the garage and he'd close them after me. Which is what I did, and we unloaded. Needless to say the vehicle went above fifty miles an hour after that!

"Others in the fellowship began to travel too: Jim and Molly, Uncle Joe and Auntie Beryl. One time we took our Anna with us; she was a little girl then. It was exciting and all a part of God's mission. Once or twice we stayed in a hotel. The service was basic, and I remember being served breakfast rolls that were as light and fluffy as concrete blocks!

"We were aware that we were under surveillance; we did our best to be discreet and bring no danger or suspicion to the local Christians. Naturally we got to know some of the contacts and pastors, but we never stayed with them. Sundays and Thursday evenings were the times the churches met, so we made sure those were our travelling days. Of course we didn't travel with our own Bibles. But it was an adventure as we watched our contacts take hold of the Bread that would be life-sustaining.

"One Sunday morning a couple of years ago, I was in a meeting in Vulcan, Romania when I saw a middle-aged lady holding a small, green New Testament. It was just like the ones we used to take in. I asked her where she got it. She told me that her parents gave it to her. I wondered whether we'd taken that one in. I have no idea, but it was encouraging to see that the Testament was still in use.

"We were travelling and working beyond our locality in Devon. While we enjoyed serving the church behind the Iron Curtain, our hearts remained fixed in the life and work of the church at Rora.

"The fellowship was about a hundred and twenty-five strong. We had appointed deacons and two more elders, making us five elders in all. Together we were leading and caring for the church, preaching God's word and aware of our purpose and identity as the body of Christ. We had a heart to see the lost saved and were seeking opportunities to share the gospel. Outwardly, everything looked good, and yet there was an unease in my spirit.

"The building work was also progressing well. With stage two reaching completion largely through Uncle Joe's unflagging commitment, we started looking at beginning the third stage – the west wing. It was to be a two-storey building comprising of an office, shop, bedrooms, bathrooms and toilets. Having taken so long to complete stage two, we felt it would be wise to ask the Lord to enable us to proceed with stage three more quickly. God confirmed this to us by the receipt of a substantial gift followed by several other gifts that meant we were able to employ a local building contractor to construct the shell. We were also able to hire a mechanical concrete pump to pump the concrete for the ground and first floor into place. In addition, a crane came and positioned the beams, unlike in the dining room where the strong Americans had lifted a single beam into position.

"We took a bank loan to erect the rafters and the roof which meant that the building was weather-proof by the winter of 1985. All the internal work of plastering, pipework and electrics we undertook to complete together as a fellowship.

"Of the three fields we'd brought from our neighbour, the field at the top of the lane was so uneven as to render it unusable. Seeing that we were still getting lots of visitors, I had a vague sense that if the field were level, campers could use it. With this in mind, and a sense that the Lord was pressing me to do this, I got a bulldozer in.

"The machine easily flattened the ground, although disaster struck when the bulldozer's goose-head arm accidentally touched the main overhead electric cable, causing the power to Liverton to be cut off. Fortunately, the driver was wearing rubber wellington boots and was unaffected by the incident.

"Within twenty minutes of this mishap, a Land Rover carrying electricians arrived at Rora. They knew exactly when and where the fault had occurred. The electricians didn't say much, but if looks could have killed… well, you get the idea.

"They informed me that we would be responsible for covering the loss of profit to the industries operating in Liverton for the duration that the electricity was off. Naturally, we agreed to pay the costs, not quite sure what they would be. In due course the bill arrived. It was for one pound.

"I also received a letter from the National Park's office in Bovey Tracey requesting that I pay them a visit. They had become aware that I had levelled one of Rora's fields. They were very polite, and just doing their job, but they informed me that I was not permitted to move substantial amounts of earth without first gaining official permission from them. I was of course ignorant of this fact and asked them rather cheekily whether they wanted me to get a wheelbarrow and a shovel and put all the earth back?

"Graciously, they said no, but advised me to put in an application for planning permission, which I did, walking out of their office praising God for His good-ness and care.

·  ·  ·

"THE CONFERENCE MINISTRY WAS ENLARGING. Norman Meeten joined us for a Young People's conference. Open Doors used our facilities for their Suffering Church weekend, and the Girls' Houseparty, which was using a school's facilities in South Devon, moved to Rora. The girls had been having their houseparty at Easter when the weather wasn't always warm, so it made sense to have the Girls' Houseparty run alongside Boys' Camp during August."

In 1984 Mr North, along with Norman Meeten, approached Malcolm and Christine to ask whether Rora would be willing to host the annual summer conference. The conference had started in 1964 at Branston camp on the Wirral. Drawing from the house churches which had begun during the early 1960s through the common link of Mr North and Norman Meeten, the group had become known as the fellowships.

By 1966 the fellowships' summer conference had outgrown Branston Camp and moved to Derbyshire where it had several locations before settling at Cliff College in Culver. Pete Gray from Liverpool, who later took on the set-up and oversight of the camp, remembers with wonder the blessings of the conference. "There was a great momentum. We were in the flow of something that God was doing. His presence was very real and many were born again, healed and delivered from oppression and evil spirits and filled with the Holy Spirit."

"When Mr North and Norman approached us," said Malcolm, "the conference was still using the Cliff College's facilities in Derbyshire. But both men felt it was time for a change of venue, and being as we were one of the fellowships, they wanted to invest the conference's resources in Rora."

In 1984 several elders from different fellowships were attending a meeting in Exeter. Since they were nearby they decided to send a survey team to Rora to see whether the grounds were suitable to accommodate the conference and its campers.

"Fifteen or more arrived," said Malcolm. "I showed them the house and we walked the fields. We stood in the middle field of the three, and Mr North asked me how much I'd charge to let them use the facilities. I informed him that I had no plan to charge them anything; we would be giving it free for the sake of the ministry.

"We knew that there was a lot to do to host the conference, but those gathered in the field that day were practical and ready to share the workload. The land, after all, was only agricultural land."

"Malcolm's right," said Pete Gray. "There was a lot of work to do. We had an architect and a surveyor in the group that inspected Rora's three fields. We quickly realised that our biggest problem was drainage. Boys' camp had used one of the fields earlier that year, and one of the leaders had dug a pit in the corner of the field. On inspection we saw that the effluent had not drained away. Malcolm said, 'He would dig a bigger pit.' One of the others who was with us commented, 'The pit would need to be the size of a swimming pool.' Malcolm joked, 'I could pump it out and spread it on my neighbour's field.'

"The engineers in the group," said Pete with a sigh, "realised that we needed to install drainage and a sewage system, which was no mean feat given that the connection to the mains sewage was nearly a mile away."

"Work on getting mains drainage and sewage to the fields began early in 1985," said Malcolm. "The Summer Conference committee raised the funds, and many brothers were involved in the process of digging and installing the pipe work ready to connect to the mains sewage at Halford Cross. We already had mains water supply in place on the edge of the newly levelled top field. Several years earlier Uncle Joe had installed a tap which enabled us to augment our own supply when it ran low. However, the house had no connection to the main sewage system. Thankfully, a generous gift changed this situation, enabling pipes to be laid up to the house at the same time as Summer Conference's sewage system was installed. This was an added blessing, as the house's septic tank was broken and we didn't have funds to repair it."

"The first summer conference was held in 1986 during the first week of August," said Pete. "My family and I arrived from Liverpool a week earlier to begin setting up the site. In the early years we used Rora's three fields as well as two belonging to the neighbour, Mr Cox. Around one thousand, five hundred people to one thousand, seven hundred attended the conference. We pitched our tent in the field. Later we marked our spot with a peg so we didn't have to measure it off each time. Sometimes we had water and sometimes we didn't, but we didn't mind. We just got on with the job. Malcolm always gave us the run of the place and was incredibly supportive.

"Officially, I had responsibility for the set-up of the conference campsite in 1979. God did give me the enabling to do it, but it was a role I grew into over the years. Initially, me and my brother-in-law Geoff Clapham used to help those who knew little about camping stay dry. We'd been Scouts and knew a thing or two about erecting tents. 'Don't use bent tent pegs or put your suitcases against the wall of the tent,' we used to tell people. It was all practical stuff, really.

"Eager to be involved, young people would accompany us from our church in Liverpool. Then their friends wanted to join us too, until the set-up team was about fifty or sixty strong. My wife Shelagh fed us all until she too had her own team of ladies helping. It was hard work, but God blessed the work. Each morning we had a prayer meeting, and that was a time of great joy and encouragement.

"Just as Malcolm was creating a platform for the ministry of summer conference to take place, the work of set-up was also giving God the opportunity to move in the main meeting tents. Therefore, we knew our heart attitudes had to be right with the Lord. This was foundational to set-up. As the whole thing grew, different fellowships took on different responsibilities, but we worked as one in unity."

"There were two large marquees on the plinth," said Malcolm. "One for the cafeteria and the other for the large meetings. When I had the vague idea of levelling the ground in that field to accommodate campers, I had no idea how the Lord was going to use it.

"Hosting the summer conference was hard work," said Malcolm. "At times there were misunderstandings, but it was great blessing too. The place was full of people. Uncle Joe used to joke, *what are all those people doing camping on my lawn*? Yet, to hear them lifting their voices in song to God in the large marquee filled me with joy."

"The Lord was moving," said Pete. "God transformed many people's lives and it was a thrill to be able to meet up once a year and hear testimonies; there are so many stories. One of the things that came out of Cliff College and continued at Rora, was the ministry of the youth tent. Norman Meeten took over that ministry, and it almost became like a mini conference within a conference. But it is staggering the number of people around the world who testify to the fact that they first met God in the youth tent at Summer Conference. There was tremendous blessing, and that blessing endures to this day. But it largely came because Malcolm and Christine had a heart to enable, encourage, and support. Malcolm's heart has always been to seek to create an environment where God's blessings can flow."

Norman Meeten and Mr North at Summer Conference

Summer Conference

# 13

# "Knowing that your labour is not in vain in the Lord"
## 1 CORINTHIANS 15:58

"We didn't have enough room in the house to accommodate the elderly at Summer Conference, and I had an idea to build dormitory type rooms that would be multi-purpose in their use. However, the National Park felt that such a building would not fit in with the style of the house, and so forth," said Malcolm with a wave of his hand. "Therefore, I took it upon myself to increase our accommodation. The Summer Conference committee covered the costs and I purchased twenty static caravans which we kept in the woods when they were not in use. I already had three, so altogether that was twenty-three.

"I had bought the caravans and sited them without the permission of the National Park. As usual, they found out about my venture. However, this time instead of sending a letter or calling me to their offices, an inspector arrived on our doorstep. He wasn't too friendly and refused to come in for coffee. But he did grant us a temporary kind of licence which enabled us to use the caravans once a year.

"We appealed, requesting permission to keep the caravans in the grounds and use them as needed. The appeal was pending and in the meantime the inspector would call in every so often to ensure that we were keeping within the guidelines. He remained distant, even refusing to shake hands. We later learned that he was married to a retired missionary but was sadly antagonistic towards Christianity and Christians. We carried on in this manner for a couple of years until we got a notice instructing us to remove the caravans by the end of that year or else the National Park's office would forcibly remove them. I can't quite remember when it was, but I know I managed to sell twenty-two of them by November, leaving us with just one.

"I decided to let them have their Christmas break, thinking if the inspector and his team hadn't come back to me at Rora by the first couple of weeks of January, then I'd visit their office and lay out my plans.

"No one came, and so I thought, 'right, here goes.' With my plans and a large map of Rora and the estate under my arm, I headed to the National Park's office. I didn't have an appointment, but everyone knew me there – my reputation proceeded me," said Malcolm raising his eyebrows. "The man I usually saw concerning plans for Rora's extensions and development hadn't returned from holiday. However, while I was in the reception area, the unfriendly inspector came in.

"'Hello, Mr Ford,' he said politely. 'What can I do for you?'

"I gestured to the plans under my arm and he invited me into their large conference room with its huge, polished table.

"'I was going to come and see you next week,' he continued.

"'Well, there's no need,' I said. 'Twenty caravans have been sold and I've sold two extra which leaves me with just one.'

"The inspector raised his eyebrows. 'You can keep that one,' he said with a smile.

"I thanked him and waited.

"'What can we do for you now?' he asked.

"Showing him my plans, I told him that I'd like planning permission for an additional building beside the dining room as the meeting hut, which they had declared unfit for use. He looked carefully at my plans and advised me to fill out an application for planning. My request would be processed in the normal way, and permission granted within six weeks.

"I marvelled that the man who had been so negative and unfriendly in the beginning ended up being warm and helpful. God transformed that man's attitude."


MALCOLM AND CHRISTINE were still travelling into Eastern Europe, although by the late 1980s they were mainly travelling to Romania with an organisation called Romanian Aid Fund. They carried Bibles but they also took in audio equipment for the churches and brought out mini cassettes that informed those in the West of the persecuted church's pledge and the unfolding political turmoil.

"The situation was worsening," said Malcolm. "Years of communist austerity were taking their toll and the populace wanted freedom and justice. Civil unrest was rising and the Securitate, the Romanian secret police who'd kept tight, brutal control of the country, were struggling. People were demanding retribution for those who'd inflicted such torment and suffering on the people.

"Despite the growing dissent, we still travelled. By then we had a growing network of contacts and friends.

"IN FEBRUARY OF 1988 A SUDDEN, unexpected death in the fellowship at Rora left us reeling. Shortly after, we had also arranged to have a week of five nights of prayer. Each evening we met in a different church members' home. By the middle of that week, for some reason I was beginning to feel uncomfortable and ill at ease. On the Thursday evening we met in a large family home in Newton Abbot. There must have been about fifty or sixty of us present. The family's lounge was packed with some people sitting in the hall, whilst others sat on the stairs.

"My unease was growing. Something, I wasn't quite sure what, was going on beneath the surface. Little by little I began to recognise what was happening. One brother was nudging the meeting in a certain direction until he was able to present his proposal to those gathered.

"He believed that the church should move from the Rora campus; that it should meet as a separate entity in another location, such as Newton Abbot. Apparently, a number of those in the fellowship felt that the building work for the growing hospitality ministry was obstructing the growth of the church, and that Rora's location was remote, making it less accessible to people in the surrounding area.

"Flabbergasted by this brother's proposal, I firmly stated my position. The church and the work were one, running according to the words that God had spoken to me. Hence, I told the meeting that I would continue to meet at Rora on Sundays. If anyone felt to come and join us, they were most welcome. But I could not accept or endorse the brother's proposal. With that, I put my Bible in my briefcase and got up to leave. Christine, Uncle Joe and Auntie Beryl followed me. Everyone else remained.

"There were further discussions, but I could not change my position: the church is the spiritual foundation of the whole. The work of Rora House is inextricably a part of the church. The ministry of the house is the ministry of the church, in accordance with the word God spoke to me in the beginning: '...*you shall be witnesses to Me in Jerusalem, and in all Judea and Samaria, and to the ends of the earth.*' ¹ We could not separate them.

"Uncle Joe also plainly stated his position, highlighting the fact that God had called him to support to me in the ministry of helps, and that he would be standing beside me.

"As the days unfolded, Christine and I began to realise that the brother's proposal had not come out of the void. Seeds had been sown, suggestions made that people had taken hold of, and so the mumblings and uncertainties had spread until the proposal was articulated.

"Two of the elders resigned and began a new church in Newton Abbot. As the brother who incited the split left, I asked him whether he had the Word of the Lord to begin a new church. He told me that he had no such word.

"Over a period of months many members of the church left. Some moved on for legitimate reasons, relocating for work or moving because of family. Some were confused and didn't know where to go or what to do, while others left to join the church that the brother had begun in Newton Abbot. A couple of months after that fateful night of prayer the fellowship had shrunk from a hundred and twenty-five members to twenty-five."

# 14

# Reconciliation, Romania, and retirement

"Church splits are devastating," said Malcolm with a sigh. "But before we proceed, I do want to highlight that there has been repentance, forgiveness and reconciliation with the brother who proposed separating the church and the work by relocating the meeting place of the church. God has graciously restored our fellowship.

"But at the time, and for several years after, we were shattered. We thought that we were a group of people in covenant relationship with God and one another. Then suddenly that was gone. Broken!" said Malcolm with sadness. "Friendships were torn apart in a moment. It felt like we'd undergone the crude amputation of a limb without anaesthetic, and our untreated wounds bled relentlessly. We grieved the loss of good friends we'd known and loved for years, and the anguish continued as further people left.

"We wanted the pain to be gone, to be able to rebuild, to move forward, but the hurt was too deep. Ease of relationships amongst those who remained had gone. We felt abandoned and betrayed. We gathered to pray, asking God to remove bitterness from our hearts and heal our souls, to let compassion guide us and not the pain we carried with us. But the grief would not be banished.

"Splits do not heal overnight, neither do they happen suddenly. For months, unbeknown to me, disquiet had been bubbling beneath the surface. A word here, a suggestion there, the gathering of people, the forming of a plan until suddenly it came into the open. I was fifty-three and merrily carrying on doing what I believed God wanted us to do. The split stopped me in my tracks. I never thought the fellowship could experience such traumatic events.

"Those who instigated the move were in some ways better leaders than me. Eloquent speakers and good Bible teachers, they exposed my lacks. Too many times to number I've mixed up my words, or failed to articulate clearly what I've meant, or worse still," said Malcolm, striking his forehead with the palm of his hand, "caused offence by speaking without thinking. And yet God had called me. He had given me His word for the work and ministry of the church at Rora and I could not lay that down.

"We might have felt like curling up and dying but we had no choice, we had to keep going. The ministry of the church continued with a steady stream of visitors and all the regular conferences and camps. People came, heard the Lord's word and returned home thanking God for Rora. It was a miracle, given the brokenness of our hearts.

"My son-in-law Mark, who's married to our daughter Rachel, remembers one incident that clearly demonstrates God's continued tender care towards us during those days. George, who took care of the grounds and worked on the large vegetable plot that kept those in the house supplied with fruit and vegetables, was struggling to keep the plants free of some sort of blight or fungus. The fungus was severely depleting our yield of crops.

"Apparently, one Sunday morning as the meeting finished, I asked the church to join me in gathering around the vegetable patch to pray that God would deal with the blight and give us a good harvest. Mark and Rachel returned to Reading and promptly forgot about this incident. It was only when they returned the following summer and Mark was walking beside the vegetable patch that he noticed the plants and bushes. Every single one was laden under the weight of healthy and plentiful produce."

BESIDE THE WORK AT HOME, God was strengthening Malcolm and Christine's links with Romania. In 1989 they made two trips and it was evident that unrest against the totalitarian regime was gathering momentum. That year was to a prove a historic year for the Romanians.

By December a small protest that started in the western city of Timisoara against government efforts to evict a Hungarian Reformed pastor ignited a movement of dissent that rapidly spread across the country. The Securitate sought to suppress the uprising, but the populace was beyond restraint. Heavy rationing and the long mismanagement of their country's resources in the face of President Ceausescu's opulent lifestyle emboldened them to act, despite the known terrors imposed on dissenters.

Depleted and diminished, the Romanian military had joined the people in their revolt against Ceausescu and his wife, Elena. On the 22nd of December, the military arrested Ceausescu and Elena trying to flee the country. Three days later they stood before military judges who sentenced them to death. Minutes after the announcement of the guilty verdict they faced the firing squad. In that moment the communism that had ruled Romania for more than forty years, toppled.

"The first week of January 1990 we packed our car with aid for the Romanian believers," said Malcolm. "Having no idea what to expect, we approached the border with a mixture of excitement and nervousness. Previously we'd waited long hours, uncertain of whether we'd get a visa stamp in our passports or not. However, this time the border guards simply welcomed us in. No one was interested in checking the contents of our car, and we smiled, thinking we could have been carrying in anything.

"The oppression was gone, there was jubilant freedom, but people didn't really know what to do with their new liberty. Food shortages continued and the West was just beginning to provide practical help, although few had any idea how grave life had been for those under Romanian Communism. We returned later in the year and things were a little more settled, but the poverty was unaltered. Their physical needs were huge. Few people had ever seen an orange, and their homes were in a terrible state of repair. Walls, both inside and out, were paint-less. Bare, broken plaster was the order of the day, and thick tape held windows and doors together. You might have a five-pound note in your pocket but you couldn't hold onto it, for their needs were so much greater than yours.

"Mind you, it was a joy to be able to meet freely and openly with our friends. Their kindness and care overwhelmed us. They would selflessly share all that they had with us, giving us a meal and going without themselves. We felt a deep love for these people and sensed that God was asking us to continue visiting and helping them.

"However, the more we visited Romania the more obvious it became that we couldn't continue living out of suitcases, neither could we impose ourselves on our Romanian friends. Others travelling from the West faced the same dilemma. We weren't quite sure what to do, but one of our early Romanian contacts, who used to receive Bibles from us, suggested we think about starting something like a hospitality centre.

"Christine and I prayed about purchasing a house in Brasov, a city in central Romania. In December 1990 we found a nine-roomed property on the market for two thousand, eight hundred pounds. We told the owner that we would return the following February with the money to purchase the house. Of course, at the point of making that pledge we had no money, but were confident that the Lord would supply the full amount. By the end of January we had received enough gifts through the post and from the fellowship at Rora to be able to buy the house.

"It was a dilapidated place in need of extensive repair, which we eventually managed to complete. It became a hospitality house for westerners travelling through Romania and a base for the unfolding ministry that God was leading us into. But of course, that's another story."

ALSO EARLY IN 1990 the Charity Commission notified Malcolm and Uncle Joe that the trustees of Rora Christian Fellowship should not be benefitting from the trust directly. For more than twenty years Malcolm, and later Uncle Joe, had been living on the property completely unaware of this ruling. Significantly, Uncle Joe was sixty-five years old on the day Malcolm visited the Charity Commissioners.

"The Charity Commissioners gave us three options," said Malcolm, starting to list them. "One, the trustees could move out and continue to come to Rora each day to carry on the work, which wasn't feasible as neither Uncle Joe nor I had any capital with which to buy a property outside Rora. Second, Uncle Joe and I could resign and we appoint new trustees, or we could pay a fee to live in the house. In truth, option two was the only practical, workable solution.

"We started the search to find and appoint new trustees. Once the new board was in place they agreed to work in conjunction with me. Uncle Joe, whose health was deteriorating, was happy to hand over his responsibilities. Both he and Auntie Beryl were tired. Uncle Joe had diabetes and we suspected that he had some other illness as well. They were ten years older than us and we recognised that it was time for them to move out.

"For twenty years they had given themselves unreservedly to us, the church and the ministry at Rora. Understanding the vision and purpose of the work at

Rora, they had served in simplicity with utter faithfulness.

"Even though Uncle Joe was an elder, he has always been a most gracious and self-effacing leader. When we travelled, he stood in my place and led because he had to, not because he aspired to.

"Many times he supported me when he may not have agreed with my thinking or my decisions. I'm not the easiest person to work with, but he obeyed the word God spoke to Him. He was my armour bearer and constantly stood at my side. As we went through the church split and weathered the aftermath, Uncle Joe took many insults, criticisms, and words of condemnation on my behalf. The arrows hit him, but he never flinched. He stood firm. He," said Malcolm with a sigh, "actually, the two of them, fulfilled the calling God gave them with great humility and love. Without their steadfast commitment Rora would not be what it is today.

"At the time we were talking about them leaving Rora, Pete and Ruth Elks and their three girls were on a year's furlough from Thailand. They had rented a cottage on Colesworthy Farm about a mile and a half from Rora and were preparing to return to Asia. The cottage would be empty and proved to be an ideal provision for Uncle Joe and Auntie Beryl. They moved in after Pete and Ruth's return to Thailand.

"As they moved out, Uncle Joe officially retired, although Auntie Beryl in her own indefatigable style continued to come over to Rora two or three days a week to do the ironing and other jobs. While they were at Colesworthy Uncle Joe received the diagnosis of a progressive supranuclear palsy, a rare brain disorder that affects movement. Their daughter Sue later helped them move to Bristol where she was able to care for them both.

"And Millie Vooght, the midwife who'd been present when I was born, died. I didn't meet her properly until later in life, when her son-in-law's second wife, Brenda, brought her to a meeting in the hut one evening. By then she was older and walked with a stick, although she was still a solid, upright woman. In introducing us, Brenda said to me, 'You don't know this lady, do you?' I agreed. I did not. 'Well, she knows you,' said Brenda. Millie went on tell me that she knew my family and that she'd been present at my birth.

"When she became a Christian I had the privilege of baptising her. She attended Rora and I watched her grow as a believer. When she died, I took her funeral. It's interesting really, she saw me into the world and by God's grace I saw her go out."

# 15

# End of era - God continues the journey

"I guess it took several years for full healing and recovery to come to the church at Rora. The restoration and the ease of deepening relationships returned slowly. Walking through the aftermath of the split we gained a clearer understanding of our own fickleness and the complete faithfulness of God and His unlimited grace. We learned much in and through this process, and by the year 2000 the fellowship was growing again. New families were joining us and old friends returned.

"All through those years we struggled with severe financial pressures too. The split not only disrupted relationships but focused our attention on the trauma we'd experienced, which caused us to neglect the proper management of funds. Consequently we had a large debt at the bank, and both the tax department and VAT office were putting pressure on us to pay our bills. It literally felt like there were difficulties on every side. Our bank manager wasn't a Christian but, sympathetic to our plight, he became our advocate and valiantly fought our corner.

"Of course, we wanted to pay our debts off and we had devised plans to do this," said Malcolm, staring down at his hands. "Every time we managed to reduce our debt, we rejoiced. By means of *our* plans, we were getting results. We thanked the Lord, but I was aware that a subtle shift had taken place in our thinking. Even though our plans were sensible, we had moved away from the word that God had spoken to us in the beginning. Thinking that we could control our finances we were formulating strategies along business lines, whereas God had asked us to wholly entrust every aspect of our lives into His hands.

"We repented and recommitted ourselves to God. The church faithfully prayed, and gradually, through a series of gifts, we cleared the debts. By 2000, for the first time in several years, we were debt-free.

"But life wasn't all bleakness. During those years the Lord continued to send workers to live in the house and be a part of the ongoing ministry. On Boxing Day 1993 a couple from Plymouth, Michael and Shirley Codner, moved into the top floor of the house with their three young children, Alice, Lucy and James. Shirley had grown up in the village and had come to Rora as a teenager.

"Incredibly practical and gifted in hospitality, Michael and Shirley were a great addition to the team living in the house. Shirley used her organisational skills to run the kitchen and provide hospitality. While Mike, as a builder, replaced windows, re-tarred the roof and built a large extension to the kitchen area that enabled us to comply with the European Union's hygiene standards.

"Life was entering a new era. The church was

steadier and growing. The church's ministry was re-established, and financially we were on a more even keel. Christine and I were getting older and less able to be involved in the day-to-day running of Rora, although we continued to bring direction and counsel to the church and its ministry.

"During those years we both experienced major health issues. In May 2003 Christine suddenly became

Michael and Shirley Codner

extremely ill with a blocked colon. She was rushed into hospital where surgeons removed a tumour which was later found to be cancerous. Thankfully, she made a good recovery, although she later experienced harrowing periods of depression.

"In 2011 I underwent heart surgery for blocked arteries. At the time this was shocking news as I'd only been suffering from mild angina, but we both had a great sense of peace. Although I was already a diabetic, the Lord quickly restored me to health following the operation.

"SEVERAL YEARS earlier Dartmoor National Park's officers, noting the deteriorating condition of the meeting hut, suggested we replace it with a permanent structure. The National Park granted us further licenses for usage of the hut, but already having planning permission to build on the end of the dining room, we decided it was time to rebuild. One National Park's officer had advised me that people liked church buildings with gothic windows and pillars. I smiled, informing him that they wouldn't get that from me. So, in June of 2004 Mike laid the foundation for the new church building.

"We had no funds specifically for the new building, but after bulldozing out the site, we gathered as a church and prayed, asking the Lord to supply our every need. As always, the church was very encouraging and supportive and many friends also gave gifts. The word in our heart again was 'brick upon brick', the same word that the Lord had given us when we began building stages one to three. It was like a continuing word in our hearts as the church building was to be an extension off the dining room.

"In September 2005, after twelve years faithful service, Mike and Shirley left Rora, and the building of the new church meeting hall came to a standstill. It stood at ground level for a while until we had funds to continue. A self-employed builder came and laid the blocks, and the work continued piecemeal. Mike did also come back and help us get some of the jobs finished.

"So many faithful workers helped us finish the work, or at least get it to the place where we could use it. For in true Rora style the hall wasn't quite complete when we held our first Christmas Carol Service on the nineteenth of December 2010. Admittedly, it was a little chilly as the electric wall heaters weren't highly effective,

but at least they took the chill off the room," said
Malcolm with a grin.

"We met in the new building with a sense of excitement and expectancy, feeling like God was going to do
something new amongst us. In one of the last meetings
we held in the hut God had spoken to me through His
word: *'The latter glory of this house shall be greater than the
former…'*[1]

"Of course, there was some sadness in vacating the
hut. That simple Red Cross hut purchased more than
forty years earlier for the grand sum of five pounds had
served us well. It was shabby when we bought it and it
didn't really improve much over the years. It had no
heating. Initially, we used to sit there wrapped up in our
overcoats. Later we got some diesel-fuelled industrial air
blowers, but they were quite smelly. The old, frosted
windows insulated with thick plastic looked sad.
Different parts of the roof leaked at different times, and
the floor was a mishmash of carpet pieces.

"We'd dug a hole in the floor and lined it with
concrete to use as our baptismal tank. Not that there
was any way of heating the water then, so folk shivered
their way through their baptismal declarations. We sat
on less than comfortable metal-framed stacking chairs.
Yet, despite the hut's scruffiness it was the place of much
blessing. Hundreds, thousands probably, gathered in that
temporary meeting place to raise their voices in worship
to God. Hundreds heard the Word of God preached
clearly, and countless people, receiving His word, saw
their lives transformed.

"It was an ordinary place, but the site of *extraordinary*
happenings, not unlike our old farmhouse kitchen at
Higher Whiddon where Christine and I knelt to receive

the baptism of the Holy Spirit. In the ordinariness of our kitchen God did something extraordinarily life changing in us. That old hut had been the same for us and many others.

"The life of the hut might have come to an end, but the life of the church has not. The hut was slowly dismantled, including the old outside toilets, the roof, and all the other externals parts. In the end we threw a huge rope around the remaining structure, tied it to the tractor, and pulled the entire thing down. Those involved in the demolition scooped up the remains and lit a giant bonfire. And that was it," said Malcolm with the click of his finger and thumb, "gone in a moment.

"The site had previously been a rose garden, although only one rose bush stood in the garden when I levelled the ground ready to position the hut. Apparently the garden had been a breeding ground for snakes, which had to be driven out or else they'd end up taking over. I couldn't help wondering how many fearful snakes God had driven out of the lives of those that met in the hut on that site over the years.

"Our new building is light, airy, and finally warm. The chairs are comfy and we feel relaxed. The bricks and mortar bring a solidness to the church, a sense of permanence to our gatherings that we never experienced in the hut. For me, that sense of permanence highlights a danger that comes to the church as it settles: we can become content. Lulled by the comfort and sturdiness of the building, our passion for adventure in God can dull. The old hut in its dilapidated state never afforded us that luxury. Shaken by the wind, the Devon rains, and endlessly in need of repair, the hut kept us mindful of the temporariness of its structure, and that reminder helped keep *me* focused on God.

"I am thankful for the new church building but I do not want to relax in it. I do not want to forget that it too is just temporary. It is the place where we as a body in Christ meet to worship Him, hear His word, and fellowship. But I do not believe God wants us to settle into a routine of church life that diverts our attention away from the work He has called us to do. We must always be awake and vigilant, listening for His voice, ready to face the challenges that our world presents to the church today.

"Fire consumed that old Red Cross hut in a moment, but it did not consume the ministry of God. I find myself waiting expectantly, looking to see what God is going to do next."

Bulldozing the garden

Praying on the site before any blocks were
laid

'Uncle' George and Peter Forbes

Many people helped. L-R Terry Higgins,
Peter Wilson, Derek Blackburn

Mike Codner laying the blocks with the help
of Andrew (in training!)

The end of an era - the hut comes down.
October 2013

Faithful brother Peter Cave came to help. He'd helped build it when it arrived at Rora, and wanted to be part of the occasion of taking it down

# 16

# 'And show me where the Christians live'

"You may think this book is a book about building buildings. But that's not the impression I want to leave you with. Every building we built was initiated by God and was built to facilitate the ministry. The growth in the physical size of Rora was always about providing an environment which could advance the teaching of God's Word and provide rest and renewal for every visitor. As I've said before, we opened the doors of Rora House and let people come in. It was a simple as that.

"Part of that ministry is naturally intensely practical: building, cooking, cleaning, and maintaining the grounds. But the important thing is, as I've sought to emphasise throughout our story, that the bedrock of the practical ministry is prayer and the Word of God. This is the priority. Rora is a demonstration of what God spoke to us, to the church, and to those He called into the work. He spoke, and what Rora is today came into being.

"But we never did it alone; God sent people to join us. We are, and always have been, part of a body of people. Some came to live in the house and be involved in the hands-on daily ministry. Out of the generosity of their hearts they contributed what they had, just like the lad who shared his food in order that Jesus might feed the five thousand. What the boy had was not enough, but in giving it into Jesus' hands it became sufficient, more than sufficient, to feed the multitude.

"God has taken our small offerings, talents and gifts and multiplied them beyond our wildest dreams.

"One of our more recent building projects demonstrates this perfectly. Summer Conference, or New Life Conference as it was renamed, annually used the plinth to pitch their two marquees on – one for the large meetings and the other for catering and dining.

"I had a growing sense that it would be good to have more permanent structures in place, first for the catering and then later for the meetings. I had in mind to construct a steel structured barn for the catering. Of course, we had no available funds at that point. However, I shared my thoughts with a couple of people. Their positive response and the gift of ten pounds in my hand encouraged me to move forward.

"The church prayed and I applied for planning permission which, miraculously, was granted immediately. The funds to complete the project started coming in and we began building. Within fourteen days we had erected the steel structure. And again, as the need arose, God sent different people to help us; everyone who came played a vital part in the construction project. A group of home educators who used to hold their training conference at Rora even came with their children for a weekend to help fix the siding timbers in place. It was a delight to see them and their children, some as young as ten years old, cutting timbers to the correct length and hammering them in place.

"We completed that project with ease. It cost thirty-seven thousand pounds and the Lord supplied every penny. But then the church was back to a place of unity and fellowship. By 2011 the plinth barn, or PB1 as it's affectionally known, was in use for the annual New Life Conference. In 2016 the conference relocated, but that hasn't mattered at all as PB1 has been, and still is, used in ways that we never could have imagined. Self-catering camping groups enjoy the facilities as do the home educators. We've had weddings and all kinds of receptions and parties in it. The village has used it for craft sales, not to mention on one occasion it was filled with children's bouncy castles one time when the weather was too wet to have them outside. That building has been a really blessing.

"But all we did was step out in faith, in obedience to God's word to our hearts. And *this* is key. Some people imagine all you need to do is open the Bible and pluck out a verse with the expectation that God will fulfil it. No!" said Malcolm. "The word must be spoken into your heart; into your very inner being so that you have a sense of knowing this is right. The Bible calls that *knowing* the witness of the Holy Spirit. Or as we call it, the 'inner witness of the Spirit'. It gives you an assurance that scripture is from God. It is a living word in my heart, or as Jeremiah described it, *a fire burning in my belly, shut up in my bones*, [1] that leaves you with no choice but to speak and to obey.

"We might not see the way forward or know the next move. But if we are willing to place our trust wholly in God, if we are willing to walk without seeing with our natural eye, to take one step and then another, we will find ourselves walking in the way of faith. This is one of the foundational principles by which Christine and I lived our lives. This is how I started, right back in the early 1960s in Ilsington Methodist chapel when those two young missioners spoke with such fervency. *'Whom shall I send, and who will go for us?'* said Alec Passmore. *'Send me,'* was my response and that response changed the course of my life, of our lives. Today I have more years behind me than in front of me, but my response is unchanged. I still say, 'yes'. I still hold the vision in my heart, still long to see the work of God flourish but it's time for others to fulfil that work.

"Not that I haven't made my mistakes. Anyone who's worked with me will tell you that I can be stubborn and don't always listen. And in those early days, because the word of God was a like a fire in my belly, I just tended to bash on with what I believed God had given me to do. At times I was brash. For instance, you couldn't carry on today with building projects as I did then.

"I started things without God's leading and guidance; I spoke without thinking. Sometimes I got into messes from which I had to repent, asking God to get me out of the chaos I'd created. There were times when I was despondent, but my heavy heart only took me back to God. My mistakes never caused me to give up. At such times the Lord spoke His word, telling me to pick myself up and hope in Him, for He was with me.

"Our mistakes do not defeat God, and they should not defeat us either. God simply uses them to teach us more about ourselves and our utter dependence on Him."

Malcolm has been called a man of faith, a man who puts faith into practice. His eldest grandson Alex describes his grandpa as a man who goes into everything with a huge heart, filled with love and care for everyone.

If you haven't met him, you might imagine that he is a giant of a man. He is not. Ageing and slightly rounded, he's a gentleman who finds it increasingly difficult to walk. He is indeed a clay pot, cracked and broken. Yet inside that old pot he carries the beautiful treasure of a life lived in Christ. He is one who has always been willing to step out and take a risk.

"I am a firm believer in the ministry of the word of God outworking in deeds," said Malcolm emphatically. "Both are equally important. It is not an option to have one without the other. Word and deed ministries are interdependent, intertwined into the whole life of the church. Some speak of the priority of the spiritual, of ensuring that we have our theology correct. I do not deny that we need to know the Lord whom we serve and His word, but some teaching can simply be cerebral and this can discourage the less academic amongst us.

"Of course we need to be wise and find the balance between good theology and faithful service. But we must remember the simplicity of the first disciples. Jesus taught ordinary people, fishermen and tax collectors, to follow Him. What they received from God they lived out daily.

"We need to do the same in our own situations and locations. We must use the resources God has given us to obey His word. The ministries of word and deed might be distinct, but they are never separate. Motivated by love for God and love for others, we seek to minister in a way that brings people to know Christ and to grow in

Him. And we do that by giving our all to God. Rejoicing in our commitment to Him and sharing ourselves and our resources with one another as a pleasing sacrifice to Him, just like the first believers in Acts chapter two.

"Christine and I learned these principles together. We learned to walk daily with God, and that has not changed. We must do the same today, believing, trusting, and obeying the word of God. Of course it is a different era; a time when our world is changing rapidly. There is much talk of political correctness and a need to respect one another's traditions and beliefs. I couldn't agree more. It is right to respect and honour one another, but we must not allow society's words against Christians to enfeeble our faith. Neither must we be bound up with rules and regulations that threaten our liberty in Christ and hold us in fear. Today is the day of salvation. Our God is the living, sovereign, almighty God. There is no other and we should preach His Word with boldness because it produces faith in us, and faith always produces good works, and good works impact people's lives.

"You may have gathered that the Wesley brothers are amongst my heroes of the faith. Well, at one time John Wesley was struggling with unbelief, and wondered whether he should stop preaching God's word. He sought the counsel of his friend Peter Bohler asking him whether he should cease preaching because he had no faith? Peter Bohler replied – 'No, Wesley should not stop but rather preach until he had faith and then, having it, he would preach faith.'

"Faith doesn't come automatically; it is a gift to receive. We must preach it, but it is not an inanimate object. It is a person: Jesus Christ, and that faith walks.

"Some have called me a radical. Perhaps I am. But the gospel we hold is radical. It goes to the core of us, addressing and dealing with the root of sin, giving us the opportunity of a completely new start. Yes! Jesus Christ is radical. The Christian life is radical, and I sense that we have a need for radical men and women of faith in this day – men and women who are willing to step out and obey God's word each day of their lives. I know that many already live this way, but there is, I believe, the need for a new move of God in our world, for those God is calling to rise and stand firm, to be willing to show the world that our God is a powerful, gracious, loving Saviour who longs to restore His kingdom amongst us.

"Years ago God spoke to me about seeing a local mission work come to birth in our area of Devon. 'Give me this valley,' was the prayer and word in my heart. That word is yet unfulfilled, but a recent conversation brought that conversation to mind. I sense the wind of the Spirit blowing, the very edge of God's ways calling, beckoning us forward as He longs to do something new amongst us.

"It is risky. It takes courage and an ability only God can give to stand firmly on His word. But I remember our own tough times, the times when we thought we would break. Those were the very moments when we understood more deeply our dependence on Him, and God never failed us.

"Perhaps you feel like me, a worn and broken vessel. I am not a clever man, I am not a professional, I have no letters after my name and yet God has used me. I am the one who has the *one* talent.

"Feelings of inadequacy should not keep us from

laying hold of the possibilities God lays before us. Instead, we must grasp them and let Him build a vision of the work for the future, a vision that changes people's lives. God calls us to look to Him. The more we do this, the more our eyes turn towards the lost. God calls the church to be the light of the world. To display a new humanity, a picture of the world to come, a challenge to the present world to submit themselves to the true King.

"This book shares a little of our story, of the blessings and of our mistakes. It is a testimony to God's goodness and the way He uses ordinary people. But I beg you, do not just read this testimony and walk away. Please ask the Lord, what He would have *you* do?

"Are you willing to respond to His question of *'Whom shall I send, and who will go for us?'* with, *'Here I am, send me!'*

"The Lord's blessing be with you all."

# Appendix

*Prophecies given by Brother North at 23, Belmont Road, Exeter in 1969.*

To Christine:

"I have a word for you, sister, will you receive it? I see the word FAITH, through all your sufferings and temptations and trials, and know this, that the Lord has devised good unto you, and He will certainly establish you greater than anything you have known before, because you are faithful."

For Christine and Malcolm, 1969, Belmont Road:

"Something further sister, will you receive it? This is to your husband as well;"

"They that have expected bad things, those that have thought that you would stumble and fall, are all of them confounded, for I have confounded them, says the Lord. And I will do unto you, that which is of My love, and not that which is of their hatred. I will do unto you exactly as I have given you to know Me in your hearts.

Therefore, fear not, for I can be no different than I am, and I will make you to be established."

*Arthur Wallis, given at the end of a conference in Rora's main lounge 1969 - 1970:*
"We will lead people to possess their possessions in Christ."

*The following is a prophecy brought by Brother North in the early 1980s. This was a general prophetic word that he gave, not just to us. It was at a brothers' meeting we had at Rora for all the brothers. The part that meant a lot to me was the paragraph that begins 'unto you I give this warning...' It is a Word to all the church, but it was significant for Christine and me too.*
"I wish to speak to you of external things. You shall go through difficult times, more difficult than you have ever known. For I say unto you, that this world will get worse and worse, and men will see no other way out than to turn unto ways that are anti-Christ, and they shall seek unto relief from this source and that. But this country shall not return unto its God; it shall seek false gods. Men shall preach though, and men shall govern the out workings of iniquity, and many of our righteous shall be shocked, even more deeply than they have ever been shocked.

"The whole world shall be driven by the devil, and so it shall come to its prophesied end. But you, My children, must not be alarmed, or to speak surprise, for I the Lord will give unto those that trust in Me, strength and courage. I will not promise you plenty, I will promise you sufficient, for I will keep My own. Some of you shall suffer, but I the Lord know your hearts; I want you to know Mine. I do not want you to turn aside unto other things; let not your heart be so troubled that you shall forsake the principles of righteousness and seek to live in unholy ways. Be distinct and separate, and when men tell you to be silent, open your mouth and speak, for there are those that must be won, for My eye is upon them too.

"Do not be overawed or dismayed and seek not unto other places. Do not forsake your own country for another, for all countries shall come under the lash of the enemy; there will be no security anywhere. Governments will not be able to fulfil promises they make and men shall be cut down during their years.

"Unto you then I give this warning; unto you I make the statement that you may abide truly in the power of the Lord; and though the church, even My church, shall be persecuted in the earth, yet shall it be a living church, and by the pressures shall the true saints of God stand forth in glory.

"Fear not then; lift your heads and your hearts, know that these are but the death throes of this age, but they shall be the birth pangs of the new. Lose not your way, but stand in that day perfect before Me, presented in all the perfections of holiness."

*Prophecy given by Brother North at Rora, Friday 7 April, 1972*

*(Last meeting of the Brethren's gathering and the sisters present. Words spoken while several of the brethren laid hand on Malcolm and Christine.)*

"Know this, that the ordination of God is upon you, and that God has chosen your path, brother and sister, and that He has put your feet on the right path. You are absolutely right, and God, even my God, shall supply all your needs according to His riches in glory. He shall supply more than your need – He shall supply the needs of those who have joined themselves to you.

"He will establish a Work on which He will write His name, and He shall pour love through this fellowship, and through this Work, that it should be a ministry unto hearts that seek love. For listen to the cries of men and women, and look around you, and you shall hear and see the cries of hearts that seek the love that is in you. Give all that you have, and I will supply all your need."

*19 May 2018 – the 50th Anniversary of Rora. Stephen Ford's speech:*

"The primary focus of this afternoon is not to think about Mum and Dad but to remember what God can do with individuals who take him at His word.

"Here are a few of my memories:

"My earliest memories are snippets of life at Ilsington Methodist Chapel where Mum and Dad attended church. At the time Dad had a farm, Higher Whiddon near Ashburton. He used to work long days, especially during the summer. Despite this they both prioritised worship, and so we children (4 of us at the time) were taken to chapel where on some occasions, especially in the evenings, we were left sleeping in the back of Dad's Ford Cortina Mk1 estate with the seats down and us lined up like sleeping lions.

"On one occasion I remember a youth event in the

chapel where there were probably 20 or 30 young people gathered for fun. My earliest memories of Whiddon were of a packed dining room with the table pushed back under the stairs, and young people crammed into every available space. Sometimes I stayed up to listen to the preaching, other times I went to bed, either way my life was impacted at an early age by the ministry and testimony of those around me.

"Having a house filled with young people was great, and I was able to interact with lots of different people. Some had motorbikes that required weekly love and attention, and so they'd be repairing them in the front yard, with oil all over the place. And there were also those who, probably under-age, were keen to test the motorbikes. Sometimes Dad would have to return them to their parents a little worse for wear from their experiences, with the assurance that it wouldn't happen again. Some of the older ones, for example John Williams (Jenny Glover and Martin Williams' Dad) would help collect bales of hay with his Morris Minor and trailer. Whatever was going on, it was never dull.

"I remember being introduced to Mr North who, when a large stone fell on my foot, was keen to intervene and take control, insisting that my foot be immersed in hot water, to draw out the swelling. At the time I thought that act was cruel but later in life I came to appreciate him; he became like a granddad to me and we enjoyed many happy exchanges. To this day I am eternally grateful to have known him.

"In summing up Rora's work and ministry I will use the acronym that Len Moules, the then International secretary of WEC, gave to Dad. Rora was the name that came with the house and it means 'house at the

bottom of the hill.' Dad asked Len, who'd been introduced to Dad and Mum by G W North, for a suggestion, or what we would call today, a strap line. Len
suggested using the name Rora as an acronym, and so
Regions Overseas, Regions Around came into being,
and that line has stuck, and probably sums up the work
and vision of Rora very well.

"Mum and Dad have big hearts and weren't afraid
to make mistakes. They believed God and took Him at
His word. It was this belief and conviction that became
the foundation and platform that equipped, launched,
and enabled many of us into sharing and equipping
others in the spiritual journey of life.

"Under the leadership and ministry of Malcolm and
Christine Ford, together with Joe and Beryl Maltby,
Rora became a launching pad and they became the
great facilitators, and through their actions and loving
care many lives were enabled and enriched to find God
and to find Him to be true and consistent.

"Dad and Mum proved that being a Christian
wasn't about what you did for Christ, rather it was about
who you are in Christ. Christ became their motivation
for the work; their heart was to see people set free and
liberated to worship the God that they had discovered.
Their testimony has been to ask, seek and to knock.

"When on the farm Dad concluded that there had
to be more to God than they were currently experiencing, and together they proceeded to expand their spiritual borders. This needs to become our experience –
one of expanding our spiritual borders, never restricting
God but embracing Him fully, and when we don't
understand then we must proceed to ask, seek and
knock. Isaiah 55:6 says, 'Seek the Lord while he may be

found, call upon Him while he is near.' As we look back, let's look forward with faith and expectancy that God is far bigger than our current experience. It has been this attitude to expand one's borders spiritually, and worked out practically, that has provided the bedrock for the faith that Christ planted in their hearts all those years ago, and it is with that faith that Christ has enabled them to work and live out their lives for over fifty years.

"When we look back as we are today, we should look at life and see the hand of God at work. Yes, we will see mistakes and failures, even unbelief and loneliness at times, but we will also see the times of being right and successful, together with belief and times of friendships, and it is in all this mixture of life's experience that we find God to be sure and steadfast.

"In looking back on the work and life of Malcolm and Christine and their faithfulness and testimony to God, who is not and cannot be restricted, let us look forward with anticipation and purpose so that our lives can be the encouragement to others that Malcolm and Christine, together with Joe and Beryl Maltby, have been to us. May the foundation of faith that was laid in our lives, because of the ministry of Rora, continue to be the foundations that enable us to live Christ. Malcolm and Christine, Joe and Beryl, and, in the very beginning, Jim and Molly Rowley, were people who stepped out of the boat, who fixed their eyes on Jesus and walked on the water. They continue to be the inspiration that enables us to live for Christ."

Christine, June 2018

*Rachel Clare at Christine's funeral:*

"What can I say in remembrance of someone of strong character?

"She was a loyal, faithful, and a constant support and champion of the cause. She had a never-ending energy that got things done.

"Lives have been touched by this dogged, single-eyed commitment. A vision has been fulfilled because someone stood shoulder to shoulder with the visionary.

"Has the journey been easy? No, sacrifices have been made, but blessings still abound. In moments of remembrance we will take time to acknowledge one who was a support when the upheld arms began to drop low; one who walked behind a sower; one who had a banquet ready. Let us remember one who is now partaking in the biggest harvest and banquet of all."

*A few comments from Jeremy Ford on Dad & Mum's personal story:*

"I think it is important to note that this is a book about the vision, mission, and God's faithfulness, and also a celebration of the unique Rora concept. The Rora vision played a very important part within the post liberal evangelical movement by placing new testament beliefs outside of the purview and control of the established religious congregation and relying solely on the direct relationship with the divine to effect real change; change within individuals, change within social and group contexts, and, more broadly, change within secular society (establishing a committed and consistent plumb line of belief, against which Rora was prepared to be judged and measured). This was clearly Dad and Mum's (and Joe and Beryl's) achievement, not the Ford family. These achievements will, I am sure, be discussed for years to come and the influence and importance will be weighed and measured. This is why it is important for it to be published (direct from the visionary)."

*Stephen Ford at Christine's funeral:*

"Mum. What can we say? Each one of us here today has a story or two or three to say about Mum, Grandma, Aunty Christine, Christine or just Chris.

"This lady, that we the Fords called Mum and Grandma, was a lady with a massive heart, a heart that was invariably worn on her sleeve, you knew what was coming next just by the expression on her face.

"It was this massive heart of hospitality that made the Ford family home into a shared home, of which I know many of you here today are appreciative of. I can't really remember a time when we didn't have someone else in our family or in our house. Mum was given to hospitality.

"Mum was born on Boxing Day, 1936 to Geoff and Phyllis Pearson (for those who remember, the infamous

PKP or Granny P, now synonymously linked with the 'Granny flat' at Rora).

"My grandparents were loving, caring and supportive parents who welcomed their eldest daughter Christine into their lives with great joy and enthusiasm, (my grandfather was 42 when mum was born). From an early age, I think it is fair to say that Christine Mary Pearson knew her own mind and had a strong sense of justice. My two aunts, Val and Kathy, have often told me that through her childhood there was this strong determination and sense that she was right, which would often lead my aunts to exaggerate the situation just to wind her up.

"Something that we as a family know about Mum is that you really had to dig deep to find any sense of humour, which is a bit ironic seeing she would meet and spend sixty years of her life with one of life's biggest joker's – my father– and there would be many a time when a joke or prank would fall flat. One such occasion was on mum's 60th birthday. Dad had modified a Zimmer frame with an old chainsaw engine mounted on a platform of wood, and wrapped it up ready for Mum to open on her birthday. It would be fair to say Mum didn't quite get the joke! Unhindered, the joker continued with his plan – what a surprise – and proceeded to take mum through a fifteen-page manual that he had written so that Mum would be able to operate this contraption with ease. The thing we remember as a family is that Dad proceeded to insist that Mum act out the manual while he read the instructions out. I am afraid we found it really funny; Mum, bless her, was less than impressed.

"Mum was born in London, and my grandparents

were in the fortunate position to provide a stable, supportive, and comfortable middle-class lifestyle. My grandfather, an engineer, had ascended through the ranks of Chrysler Dodge and by the time World War II had broken out had become the works manager of the factory based in Kew, London. My grandfather had been brought up in a comfortable, middle-class family, an only child to parents who were in a fortunate position of being able to send him to a private boarding school, Queens college, Taunton for his education. My grandmother, the infamous PKP, was born in India to a Methodist missionary and spent most of her young life either at boarding school in England or with an aunt. She met and married Geoff in 1934, and together they set about providing the loving, caring family home that Mum grew up in.

"At some point the family moved to New Malden in Surrey and Mum attended Tiffin Girls in Kingston where she gained her O-Levels.

"During her teenage years Mum attended Girl Guides, and it was through this organisation that she began to explore Christ. I am sure that Granny P talked to her about Christianity and its values, but Mum had this insatiable desire to find out more, believing that Christianity was more than just good morals and values.

"I am not sure of the details, but at some point in those teenage years Mum attended a camp at Capernwray in Lancashire, and it was there under the ministry of Major Ian Thomas that Mum made her commitment to Christ, something that made a lasting impression on her.

"My recollection, from what I was told, is that she started A-Levels but then went into a nursing career at

St Bart's hospital, and it was here that she met my mother-in-law, Jennifer Dale. A friendship between the Dales and Fords was started that has lasted sixty years.

"So, how come she met Dad, this London girl, and this Devon farmer, I hear you ask? Well, she joined the Christian union, and as far as I know it was from this group that a group of four girls decided to go on holiday together in Devon. They planned to hitchhike from London to Devon, but my grandfather would not allow her to hitchhike, so agreed to her travelling on the train with the luggage.

"So the three girls set off on their journey whilst the fourth sat on a train. Don't ask me about the logistics in the days before mobile phones. All I know is that a young man in a flashy Ford Anglia 100e, picked up these three young ladies and drove them to their destination and there met the fourth member of the group who had arrived with the luggage. I was told by Mum that this young man appeared later in the week bearing gifts of farm produce and wine for these girls, obviously keen to impress. Mum went home, quit her nursing career for a job as a nanny in South Devon, and moved herself, much to her family's disapproval, to Devon. This young man proposed, and in March 1958, sixty years ago, Christine Mary Pearson became Christine Mary Ford, and so the real story begins.

"If we were to sum up Mum's life it would be fair to say that she was strong-willed, determined, and had a strong sense of justice with a big heart that enabled Dad and Mum together to make themselves and their home available to many. It was this selfless act of denying herself the comfort and security of her own home and her family that led to a life that has selflessly served others, via a means of hospitality that has enriched so many lives here and abroad, especially Romania. Romania became her second home. She learned the language so that she was able to share the gospel with the poor and needy, and with Dad's help, provided the needed material help in the form of food and furniture, which lead to education and friendship for many a gypsy family.

"Without Mum's support and commitment to Dad and the vision that was given him by God for his life's work, many of us would not be where we are today in Christ. I would say that this decision, support, and commitment that Mum has exhibited throughout her life has not been without its cost, especially on us as a family. We shared our mum with the world, sometimes not by choice. There have been times when we would have loved to have her to ourselves but life is not all about me and what I want, it is about God, His wonderful creation, and this gift of life eternal that we get to experience for a fleeting moment here on this earth. Let's not waste our time here on earth; Mum didn't, every minute counted for Jesus.

"Let us remember Mum, Grandma, Christine, Chris, and Dear with an affection and appreciation of a life well lived in the service for others. May we remember a lady who always meant well and who dili-gently and steadfastly gave up all she wanted or dreamed of in order that many could find a home. I give you the life and testimony of the formidable force that is Mum, Grandma, Aunty Christine, Christine, Chris, and Dear. A life lived in the service of her Lord and for the glory of God."

# Notes

## 1. When an heir of salvation was born

1. Creation of a new word.

## 2. "Here I am, send me!"

1. Acts 2:38-39
2. Maid – Devonian expression for a lady, usually young.
3. Isaiah 6:8
4. Acts 19:2
5. Matthew 7:7a

## 3. Tears upon the flagstones

1. WEC- Worldwide Evangelisation for Christ.
2. Assistance given by Ronald Bailey, pastor of New Covenant Church Bracknell, in the wording of this paragraph.
3. See appendix for full prophecy.

## 4. Walking on the water

1. 2 Corinthians 6:14
2. 2 Corinthians 6:17
3. Revelation 18:4
4. Hebrews 10:25
5. Matthew 18:20

## 5. Reality sets in and the journey begins

1. Isaiah 6:8

## 7. Happy the souls that first believed

1. Proverbs 29:18

## 8. And kindly help each other on

1. 1 Samuel 14:7.
2. Ancient Lights or The Right to Light law, (established in England in 1663) considered it an essential health requirement that all homes receive natural daylight. The law forbids builders from constructing properties that had obstructing windows on buildings that had been standing for twenty years or more.
3. Isaiah 54:2-3

## 10. Brick upon brick. Faith – a bag of cement

1. Isaiah 28:13

## 13. "Knowing that your labour is not in vain in the Lord"

1. Acts 1:8b.

## 15. End of era – God continues the journey

1. Haggai 2:9

## 16. 'And show me where the Christians live'

1. Jeremiah 20:9

# Acknowledgments

A book is never written by one person. And that is certainly true in this case. In my efforts to tell something of our story and the story of Rora I have contacted several people, all of whom have helped jogged my memory, which isn't what it used to be. I may still have muddled dates and the sequence of events, but I trust that you will excuse those mistakes and see beyond to the story that God has woven into our lives.

I would like to thank the following people for their help and contribution: John and Cherry Balchin, Keith Challen, Mark Clare, Mike Coles, Ruth Elks, Chris French, Pete Gray, Gordon and Chrissy Harvey, Bob and Marg Jones, Vee Lacey, Rick Maltby, Dave Medlock, Pearl Page, Alec Passmore, Mark Pool, Chris Stoneman, Robin and Celia Talbot, Anna Wilkins, Martin Williams and Sue Woolnough. Fiona Harrison and Lee-Anne Brinklow respectively, thank you for your edits and proofreading. And if I have forgotten anyone, then I apologise.

A special note of thanks to Steve, my eldest son who continues to encourage his old dad. Thank you to Anna and Paul who care for me along with all the folk at Rora.

Finally, I am thankful to the Lord for giving me such a wife as Christine who stuck with me, loved me, and supported me in every way during our long and amazing marriage. And naturally, I thank God for His incredible and continued salvation of a sinner like me.

Great is Thy faithfulness, O God my Father
There is no shadow of turning with Thee
Thou changest not, Thy compassions,
they fail not
As Thou hast been, Thou forever will be

Great is Thy faithfulness
Great is Thy faithfulness
Morning by morning new mercies I see
All I have needed Thy hand hath provided
Great is Thy faithfulness, Lord, unto me